Foreign Exchange Markets

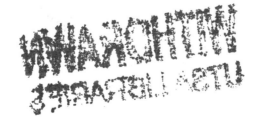

FOREIGN EXCHANGE MARKETS

Brian Coyle

Glenlake Publishing Company, Ltd
Chicago • London • New Delhi

AMACOM
American Management Association

New York • Atlanta • Boston • Chicago • Kansas City • San Francisco • Washington, D.C.
Brussels • Mexico City • Tokyo • Toronto

This book is available at a special
discount when ordered in bulk quantities.
For information contact Special Sales Department,
AMACOM, an imprint of AMA Publications, a division of
American Management Association,
1601 Broadway, New York, NY 10019

ISBN: 0-8144-0612-2

Printing number

10 9 8 7 6 5 4 3 2 1

Contents

Introduction to the Foreign Exchange Markets

International trade creates a need for buying, selling or borrowing foreign currencies. When, for example, an exporter in Japan sells goods to a customer in the US, the sale will be priced in yen, dollars, or perhaps a third currency such as sterling.

- **If** the sale is priced in yen, the customer will purchase yen with dollars in order to make the payment.
- **If** the sale price is in dollars, the Japanese supplier normally will wish to convert the receipts into his domestic currency, yen, and will sell dollars in exchange for yen.
- **If** the sale price is in a third currency, such as sterling, the customer will buy sterling in exchange for dollars to make the payment and the supplier will then sell the sterling in exchange for yen.

On occasion, international trade transactions do not result in the sale or purchase of foreign currency because companies either have foreign currency bank accounts for receipts and payments, or might pay for a purchase with a foreign currency bank loan.

Buying and selling currencies, depositing foreign currency in a bank and currency borrowing and lending are all financial market activities that in turn support international trade.

Currency is bought and sold in foreign exchange markets that are commonly referred to as FX or y

Foreign currency lending and borrowing takes place in the eurocurrency markets. Together, the FX markets and the eurocurrency markets make up the foreign currency cash markets.

Currencies also are traded in other forms as derivative instruments, such as currency swaps, options and futures. These are more sophisticated instruments for trading in foreign currencies that are derived from an underlying foreign exchange market or eurocurrency market transaction, and were first devised during the 1970s.

The Currency Markets

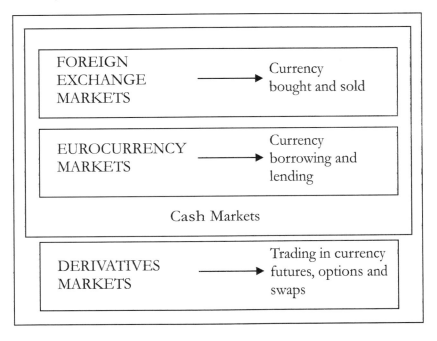

Exchange Rates

The price at which one currency is traded in exchange for another in the FX markets is the exchange rate between the two currencies. In a free market these prices move up or down according to demand and supply, whereas in regulated markets exchange rates are controlled. FX markets for the major traded currencies are partially regulated to the extent that some governments try to stabilize the exchange rate for their domestic currency against other major currencies. For example, the government of a developing country might try to achieve a stable rate for its currency against the dollar.

To a large extent, however, the main FX markets are now fairly free from controls, and exchange rates between the major currencies, most notably the dollar, the yen and the euro, fluctuate freely according to demand and supply.

Currency Risk

Fluctuations or *volatility* in exchange rates cause currency risk.

In brief, currency risk is the risk that adverse movements in exchange rates will reduce the anticipated income or increase the anticipated expenditure of any company that buys, sells, borrows or lends foreign currency. The size of a company's exposure to currency risk depends on the volume of its income, expenditure, borrowing or lending in each currency.

For example, suppose that a UK company has spent £1 million on a contract to supply a US customer, and the contract price is $2 million. If the exchange rate is £1 = $1.60, the company can expect to sell its dollar receipts for £1.25 million and realize a profit of £250,000 on the contract when the customer eventually pays. Until payment is received, the company has an exposure of $2 million in receivables and it is at risk of a weakening of the dollar against sterling. When payment is received, the exchange rate might be £1 = $1.80, and the company's income of $2 million would then be worth just £1.111 million. The anticipated profit of £250,000 will become a much lower profit of about £111,000.

The exchange rate could move favorably as well as adversely. If the exchange rate on receipt of the $2 million in this example were £1 = $1.50, the dollar revenue would be sold for £1.333 million to realize a profit on the contract of £333,000.

A key aspect of currency exposures is that although a company might wish to make a planned profit, or incur a certain cost, from its international selling or buying, currency exposures and exchange rate movements can put the plan at risk. Profits or losses can become more dependent on exchange rate changes than on the inherent profitability of the underlying trade in goods or services.

Currency risk is made much greater when exchange rate movements are potentially large and unpredictable. In other words, volatile exchange rates make currency risks more severe.

Hedging Currency Exposures

Exposures to currency risk can be reduced or even eliminated by hedging. The aim of hedging is to ensure, so far as is possible, that profits or costs are more predictable and thus less susceptible to exchange rate variability.

One commonly used instrument for hedging currency exposures is the forward exchange contract, a foreign exchange market transaction. The FX markets are not just a means of buying or selling currency, they also can be used to obtain protection against adverse future movements in exchange rates.

Currency Risk Management and Hedging

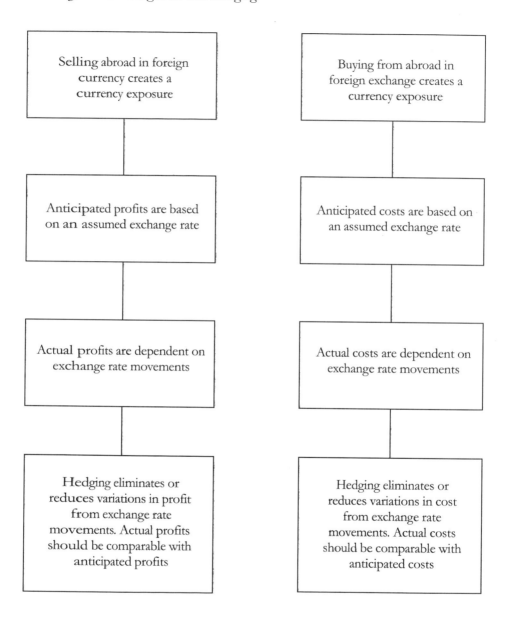

Selling abroad in foreign currency creates a currency exposure	Buying from abroad in foreign exchange creates a currency exposure
Anticipated profits are based on an assumed exchange rate	Anticipated costs are based on an assumed exchange rate
Actual profits are dependent on exchange rate movements	Actual costs are dependent on exchange rate movements
Hedging eliminates or reduces variations in profit from exchange rate movements. Actual profits should be comparable with anticipated profits	Hedging eliminates or reduces variations in cost from exchange rate movements. Actual costs should be comparable with anticipated costs

2

How FX Markets Are Structured

A foreign exchange transaction is a contract to buy or sell a quantity of one currency in exchange for another at a specified time for delivery and settlement, and at a specified price or rate of exchange. These transactions take place in the foreign exchange markets.

Origins of FX Markets

The origins of these markets lie in the execution of foreign exchange transactions for immediate value. Such transactions have taken place for several centuries, often with gold as an intermediary measure of value. Although the UK finally left the gold standard in 1931, the sterling/dollar rate remained fixed. An international system of fixed exchange rates with occasional realignments of currencies, known as the Bretton Woods Agreement, operated after World War II until 1971, when the US abandoned the gold standard. The pressures that forced the US action were also responsible for the progressive collapse of fixed exchange rates and the flotation of the major currencies in the early 1970s.

Once currencies were free to respond to changes in economic fundamentals by adjusting their relative values, a mechanism for executing large FX transactions became necessary. This was the creative stimulus behind the foreign exchange market that flourishes today.

Under the previous system of fixed rates with infrequent realignment of currencies, companies had few losses caused by an adverse currency movement. For example, a British company selling in the US in the 1950s knew that the dollar proceeds could be exchanged at a rate of about £1 = \$4 when they were received weeks or months later. It was only when currencies started to float that losses due to adverse exchange rate movements became a problem that in turn demanded a solution.

The Market Place

Some financial markets have a physical center. Some futures markets, for example, have a trading floor where dealers meet to transact their trades. Most stock markets no longer have a trading floor, but they do have a headquarters building and so a physical center. In contrast, the FX markets have no central trading forum or any headquarters. They consist of FX dealing rooms within banks and companies that trade by telephone and computer.

The FX markets are operated by banks around the world, in all countries where currency trading is not prohibited by government regulations on exchange controls. Within each country, there is likely to be a single FX center, where all banks conducting FX dealing activities locate their dealing center.

Most foreign exchange trading is conducted between banks. Non-financial companies wishing to make foreign currency transactions will either

- deal with a bank, or
- in the case of companies within the same group, have internal procedures for inter-company currency trading.

Major international banks trade in many currencies from offices in several countries. Other banks specialize in certain currencies. For example, Swedish banks will specialize mainly in krona trading, hoping to attract a large proportion of the buying and selling orders for their currency.

A bank will want to be a major dealer in a particular currency, in any country, only if its trading profits are sufficient to support the costs of its dealing operation. The bank will employ a dealer or dealers with responsibility for deciding the exchange rate at which the bank will buy or sell the currency at any time. Trading profits represent the difference between the prices at which they buy and sell currencies. Exchange rate movements occur because dealers must adjust their prices continually to match buying and selling demand.

Despite its lack of a physical center, the FX market is still a market, in the sense that it is a system for bringing buyers and sellers together and for supplying information about prices and trading activity to participants. The dealers responsible for setting the prices at which their banks will exchange currencies must have access to the latest prices in the market. This information is provided constantly by computer networks and brokers.

The global foreign exchange market has established three principal dealing centers, each operating within a specific time zone, in London, New York and Tokyo. Historically London has been the major center for foreign exchange trading, a Bank of England survey of FX markets in 1998 confirmed London's leading position by showing that it accounted for 32% of global FX markets.

FX Daily Turnover in $

Dealing center	$ billion
UK	637
US	351
Japan	149
Singapore	139
Germany	94
Switzerland	82
Hong Kong	79
France	72

Source: *Bank of England Quarterly Bulletin, November 1998*

Currencies Traded

The dollar is the cornerstone of the foreign exchange market. This reflects

- the role of the dollar as the favored currency of major energy and agricultural commodities
- the power of the US economy and its central role in the world economy
- the dollar's status as the traditional reserve currency, and a safe haven for investors in times of world crisis.

However, worldwide trading in yen has increased in volume, and the euro came into existence in January 1999, two currencies that may challenge the supremacy of the dollar.

Every currency is quoted against the dollar, and most currency transactions include the dollar as one of the two constituent currencies. In 1998 about 15% of trades in London were in sterling/dollar and about 20% in dollar/deutschemarks. The other two major currencies are the Swiss franc and the yen.

Most non-dollar transactions are called cross-currency deals and involve two transactions, a purchase and a selling transaction in exchange for dollars. A Swiss franc/yen exchange, for example, would be a cross-currency deal, involving the bank in two transactions, dollar/yen and dollar/Swiss franc.

Cross-Currency Deal

Aim

| Sell Currency A |
| Buy Currency B |

Effected by

| Sell Currency A | → | Sell dollars |
| Buy dollars | | Buy Currency B |

If a bank transacts the purchase of a large quantity of Swiss francs in exchange for yen, it would sell yen and purchase Swiss francs for dollars in two separate transactions.

There are two types of FX transaction

- trade transactions, between a bank and a non-bank customer, where the customer wishes to buy or sell a quantity of currency to complete a trading transaction or, occasionally, speculates for profit by anticipating future changes in the exchange rate, and
- inter-bank transactions, where two banks trade currencies between themselves.

Banks buy and sell huge quantities of foreign currencies. They also accept currency deposits and lend in foreign currency. In much the same way that non-bank companies take on currency exposures with their international trading, banks also have exposures if they sell more or less of a currency than they buy.

A small percentage of foreign exchange transactions are trade-related. Dealing by financial institutions such as insurance companies and pension funds with overseas investments also accounts for some turnover in the market. The great majority of FX deals by value are transacted between banks. This is partly to hedge their exposures to customer business, but by far the greatest part of the interbank market is speculative trade.

Time Zones

The trading times of the three major FX markets effectively spans 24 hours. Expressed in local time, the approximate unofficial dealing hours of each FX center are

London	8.00-16.30
New York	8.30-16.30
Tokyo	8.00-17.30

The major banks deal in all three centers and are prepared to execute customer orders throughout the day or night. The gap between the close of New York and the opening of Tokyo is usually covered by extended hours at a bank's dealing rooms.

Exchange Rate Movements

The factors that influence market demand and supply for a currency, and so move exchange rates, can be divided into long-term and short-term influences. Long-term factors are economic and regulatory conditions that create the demand for buying or selling a currency for trading or investment purposes. The average exchange rate between two currencies over time, and changes in this exchange rate, should reflect the differing conditions in each country.

Short-term factors are influences on demand and supply arising out of immediate conditions in the FX markets that should not persist for the long term. A temporary shortage of sellers in any currency will drive up the currency's price to attract sellers to the market. Market sentiment might create expectations of a fall or rise in a currency's value. If this results in speculative or precautionary buying or selling of that currency, its exchange rate might shift substantially in the short term, and perhaps for periods of several days, weeks or even months.

Factors Influencing Currency Demand

Long Term
- Balance of trade on currency account. Foreign trade in goods and services creates demand for currencies to pay for them.
- Inflation rate. A higher rate of inflation will make a country's currency less attractive because of the loss of real value with inflation.
- Economic conditions and related political conditions. Strong

economies attract more investors and increase demand for the currency.

- Interest rates. In the long term, high interest rates may be required to maintain the value of a high-risk currency. Even so, a currency with high interest rates is expected to decline in value against lower-yielding currencies over the longer term.

Short Term

- These continuous variations are influenced by short-term supply and demand conditions, and in particular by market sentiment, itself a function of regular re-evaluation by market players of the cocktail of the long run factors described above.
- Interest rates. An increase in interest rates will attract more investment from abroad; investors will sell other currencies to buy investments in the currency now offering a higher yield.
- Expectation versus realization. Even if economic news is good, the currency may fall if the news is not so good as expected. The reverse also applies. For example, the dollar could rise in value against other currencies if an expected fall in interest rates did not occur, or if a balance of payments deficit were lower than expected.
- Government intervention. To some extent, governments and central banks can intervene in FX markets to influence the exchange rate of their currency. In some cases, governments might co-operate to influence the value of a particular currency by buying or selling it using their official currency reserves.

Spot Transactions

3

A foreign exchange transaction to buy or sell currency is either a *spot* transaction or a *forward* transaction. A spot transaction is a contract to buy or sell a quantity of a foreign currency for immediate settlement or value. The exchange rate for a spot transaction is known as the spot rate.

Value Date for Spot Transactions

Currency transactions for immediate value traditionally require two banking days' notice before settlement. When a spot transaction is made on the dealing date, the exchange of currencies will occur two working days later. Settlement date is known as spot value date because that is the day when the exchanged currencies are delivered with good value into the bank accounts of the counterparties to the transaction. This allows time for the necessary paperwork and cash transfers to be arranged. These arrangements consist of

- the verification of the transaction, through an exchange of confirmations between the counterparties, detailing the terms of the deal
- the issue of settlement instructions by each counterparty to its bank to pay the contracted amount on the appointed date
- satisfying exchange control requirements where these exist.

When one counterparty is a bank, payment may be made by its own branches or by another bank acting as agent. The actual transfers of funds will be carried out on the value date.

Spot Transactions: Dealing Date and Value Date

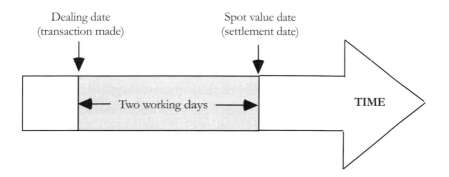

Working days do not include Saturdays, Sundays or bank holidays in either of the countries of the two currencies involved. A spot deal transacted on a Tuesday, for example, will be settled on the Thursday of the same week and a deal agreed on a Friday will be settled on the following Tuesday.

There are some exceptions. For example

- a transaction for dollars against Canadian dollars is usually for delivery on the next working day. This is referred to as funds
- FX markets in the Middle East are closed on Fridays but open on Saturdays. A transaction involving the exchange of dollars and Saudi riyals could have a split settlement date, the dollars being delivered on the Friday and the Saudi riyals on the Saturday.

Spot Rates

Interbank spot rates are the current selling and buying prices for spot transactions in a currency,

- they are used for foreign currency transactions above a certain size, and
- they provide the basis for an exchange rate for transactions of smaller sizes.

For example, if a company wishes to buy $5 million spot, its bank will quote the current interbank spot rate for the transaction. However, if the company wished to buy $50,000, the bank would quote a rate less favorable to the customer, although still based on the interbank rate, in order to obtain a reasonable profit from a relatively small transaction.

The minimum transaction size at which a bank will be willing to deal at the interbank spot rate varies with currencies and individual banks.

Spot rates are quoted as one unit of base currency against a number of units of variable currency. Quoted rates are the rates at which a bank will buy or sell the base currency: for example £1 = $1.6105 for sterling/dollar or $1 = ¥122.510 for dollar/yen.

$$\underline{\text{Base currency}} = \underline{\text{Variable currency}}$$
$$\text{1 unit} \qquad \text{?? units}$$

Spot rates are published in daily newspapers. The *Financial Times*, for example, shows the spot rates for the major trading currencies against the dollar and the euro at the close of the London FX market the previous day. Price quotations are illustrated in the tables on pages 19 and 20.

There are two spot rates for a currency, a *bid rate* and an *offer rate* that are explained in more detail later. As the bank and the customer are counterparties, they are on opposite sides of the transaction. If a US manufacturing company is converting the proceeds of product sales into Japan by *selling* yen for dollars, the bank is then *buying* yen for dollars.

Prices shown for euro spot rates indicate the exchange rate for each currency per euro. Similarly, prices for dollar spot rates are the exchange rate for each currency per dollar, with the exception of the euro and sterling that are shown as the number of dollars per euro and per pound.

- The closing mid-point is mid-way between the bid and offer rates for the currency, i.e. the rates at which the bank buys and sells the base currency respectively.
- The bid/offer spread shows the last three decimal points of the bid rate and the offer rate respectively.

Euro Spot

May 17		Closing mid point	Bid/offer spread	Day's mid high	low
Europe					
Czech Rep	(Koruna)	37.6134	924 – 343	37.6500	37.5580
Denmark	(DKr)	7.4342	317 - 366	7.4366	7.4317
Greece	(Dr)	325.331	110 - 552	325.552	324.723
Hungary	(Forint)	250.329	175 – 482	250.550	249.240
Norway	(NKr)	11.1410	357 - 462	11.1515	11.1035
Poland	(Zloty)	4.1894	870 - 918	4.1962	4.1825
Romania	(Leu)	16306.07	166 - 047	-	-
Russia	(Rouble)	26.4420	730 – 110	26.7917	25.4324
Slovakia	(Koruna)	46.3087	002 – 172	45.9009	42.3274
Sweden	(SKr)	12.3663	547 - 779	12.4060	12.2870
Switzerland	(SFr)	2.1952	937 - 966	2.1975	2.1850
Americas					
Argentina	(A)	1.0674	671 – 676	1.0685	1.0640
Brazil	(Cr)	1.7795	781 – 809	1.7815	1.7687
Canada	(C$)	1.9458	447 - 468	1.9650	1.9400
Mexico	(Peso)	9.9993	921 – 065	10.0137	9.9609
USA	($)	1.4805	800 - 810	1.4840	1.4770
Pacific/Middle East/Africa					
Australia	(A$)	2.1653	637 - 668	2.1880	2.1630
Hong Kong	(HK$)	11.4354	300 - 407	11.4630	11.4100
Japan	(¥)	166.401	322 - 479	166.590	165.210
Malaysia	(M$)	4.0565	697 – 716	4.0605	4.0445
New Zealand	(NZ$)	2.6344	311 - 376	2.6520	2.6300
Philippines	(Peso)	40.5650	040 – 260	40.6640	40.3864
Saudi Arabia	(SR)	4.0037	028 – 046	4.0082	3.9913
Singapore	(S$)	1.8276	267 – 284	1.8287	1.8238
South Africa	(R)	6.6132	013 – 251	6.6520	6.5917
South Korea	(Won)	1288.21	770 - 871	1296.87	1287.70

Dollar Spot

May 17		Closing mid point	Bid/offer spread	Day's mid high	low
Europe					
Denmark	(DKr)	6.9641	631 - 651	6.9819	6.9573
Greece	(Dr)	304.760	610 - 910	305.940	304.440
Norway	(NKr)	7.6835	800 - 870	7.7109	7.6740
Sweden	(SKr)	8.4190	140 - 240	8.4344	8.3905
Switzerland	(SFr)	1.5008	005 - 010	1.5079	1.4991
UK	(£)	1.6200	196 - 204	1.6215	1.6148
Euro	(€)	1.0675	673 - 677	1.0687	1.0642
Americas					
Argentina	(A)	0.9999	998 – 999	0.9999	0.9998
Brazil	(Cr)	1.6670	660 – 680	1.6680	1.6620
Canada	(C$)	1.4597	592 - 602	1.4679	1.4595
Mexico	(Peso)	9.3670	620 - 720	9.3720	9.3600
Pacific/middle east/Africa					
Australia	(A$)	1.5023	015 - 031	1.5113	1.5011
Hong Kong	(HK$)	7.7523	520 - 525	7.7525	7.7520
India	(Rs)	42.7300	000 - 600	42.7720	42.7000
Japan	(¥)	123.160	120 - 200	123.370	122.850
Malaysia	(M$)	3.8000	500 - 500	3.8002	3.7998
New Zealand	(NZ$)	1.7881	867 - 895	1.7960	1.7867
Saudi Arabia	(SR)	3.7506	504 - 507	3.7507	3.7504
Singapore	(S$)	1.7120	115 - 125	1.7160	1.7105
S Africa	(R)	6.1950	850 - 050	6.2350	6.1850
South Korea	(Won)	1206.75	650 - 700	1213.50	1206.50
Taiwan	(NT$)	32.7845	810 - 880	32.7880	32.7400
Thailand	(Bt)	37.2300	800 - 800	37.3550	37.2500

Example 1

The closing mid-point for the euro spot against Swedish krona in the table is 8.9873, and the bid/offer spread is 803-943.

Analysis

This means that the banks will buy and sell krona against euros as follows

Bid rate		Offer rate
(Bank buys) 8.9803	Mid-point 8.9873	(Bank sells) 8.9943

Example 2
The closing mid-point for the South African rand against the dollar (spot) in the table is 6.1950, and the bid-offer spread is 850-050.

Analysis
This means that the banks will buy and sell rands against the dollar spot as follows

Bid rate		Offer rate
(Bank buys) 6.1850	Mid-point 6.1950	(Bank sells) 6.2050

Selling and Buying Rates
A bank quotes two exchange rates,

- the rate at which the customer can buy the quoted currency in exchange for the base currency (bid rate), and
- the rate at which the customer can sell the quoted currency in exchange for the base currency (offer rate).

The terms bid and offer can be confusing and it is easy to mix them up. They originate from inter-bank transactions that are mainly against the dollar. The bid rate is the rate at which the bank is willing to pay to buy dollars and sell the non-dollar currency, and the offer rate is the rate at which the bank will offer to sell dollars and buy the non-dollar currency.

The bank will always buy and sell currency at the more favorable of these two rates to itself. The difference between the two rates is known as the *spread*, sometimes the bid-ask spread and the bid-offer spread in the UK.

Guidelines
Buying and selling rates are easily confused because in any foreign currency transaction Party A is selling what Party B is buying, and vice versa.

Exchange rate *	Quoted currency (variable)	Base currency
Sterling/Swiss franc (£/SFr)	2.4302-2.4322	per £1
Dollar/Japanese yen ($/¥)	123.120-123.200	per $1
Euro/Canadian dollar (€/C$)	1.5574-1.5591	per €1

*By convention the base currency is written first and the variable currency second.

Taking the variable currency

- if the customer is buying the variable currency, he will be quoted the lower rate (bid rate), and
- if the customer is selling the variable currency, he will be quoted the higher rate (offer rate).

The key concept is that a bank will quote two rates, one for buying and one for selling, and the rate for any transaction is the one that is more favorable to the bank.

Base currency A

Quoted currency B – rates against base currency (i.e. B Units per unit of A)

Bid — Bank buys base currency and sells variable currency

Offer — Bank sells base currency and buys variable currency

[Rule: The exchange rate is the price of the base currency in terms of quoted currency. The bank always will pay a lower price for the base currency and sell it at a higher price. Hence the bid rate is always lower than the offer rate.]

Example

A UK customer wants to buy $750,000 from a bank in exchange for sterling. The bank quotes the following rates: £1 = $1.6200-1.6210. The customer is buying dollars for sterling, and sterling is the base currency in this case. The rate for this transaction is therefore the bid rate, 1.6200. The cost of the dollars will be £462,962.96 ($750,000 ÷ 1.6200).

Another customer wants to sell $750,000 to the bank that quotes the same rates. Because the customer is selling dollars for sterling, the rate for this transaction is the offer rate, 1.6210, and the bank will pay £462,677.36 ($750,000 ÷ 1.6210) for the dollars.

The spread between the two quoted rates, bid and offer, gives the bank its profit on its FX dealings. Here, a simultaneous purchase and sale of $750,000 at the quoted rates would produce a profit for the bank of £285.60.

Points

Most exchange rates are quoted up to four decimal places. The sterling/dollar rate, for example, is taken to 0.0001 of a dollar (0.01 cents). The last two numbers are referred to as *points*. For example, if the sterling/dollar (£/$) rate alters from $1.5955 to $1.5965, the rate will have gone up, with the dollar weakening against sterling, by ten points.

FX dealers making large transactions between themselves usually will quote just the points digits to each other, assuming that everyone knows the main figures in the exchange rate. For example, a bank might quote a price of 60-65 to a large corporate dealer, and both will know that this means $1.6160-1.6165 when the dollar is trading between 1.61 and 1.62. If the market rate were to be $1.6100-1.6110 this would be quoted as figure – 10, the assumption being that both parties know the exact number of cents.

Exercises

To gain familiarity with spot exchange rates, determine the correct answers to the following problems.

Spot rate: euro against

Dollar	1.0571-1.0575
Swiss franc	1.5935-1.5946
Yen	131.40-131.54

Assume that these spot rates would apply to each problem.

Problem 1

A German company has to make a payment of $400,000 to a supplier. What price would the bank quote in euros for the dollars?

Problem 2

A French company wishes to convert the SFr600,000 it has just received from a Swiss customer into euros. How much would the bank be willing to offer?

Problem 3

A Spanish importer of electrical goods from Japan must pay ¥45 million to a supplier. At what price in euros would the bank fix the foreign exchange transaction with this customer?

Solutions

Problem 1

The bank is selling dollars and buying euros and the spot rate is therefore the bid rate for the base currency (euro) that is 1.0571.

The customer will have to pay €378,393.72 (400,000 ÷ 1.0571) for the dollars.

Problem 2

The bank is buying Swiss francs and selling euros and the spot rate is therefore the offer rate for the base currency (euro), 1.5946.

The customer will obtain €376,269.91 (600,000 ÷ 1.5946) in exchange for the Swiss francs.

Problem 3

The bank is selling yen and buying euros and the spot rate is therefore the bid rate for the base currency (euro) 131.40.

The customer will have to pay €342,465.75 (45 million ÷ 131.40) for the yen.

Direct and Indirect Quotations

There are two ways of quoting exchange rates, direct and indirect.

- For direct quotation, the value of one unit of the foreign currency is expressed in terms of the domestic currency. For example in the UK, the rate for the euro against sterling might be stated as £0.6678 per euro.
- For indirect quotation, a foreign currency's value is expressed in terms of one unit of domestic currency. For example, the sterling/euro rate could be quoted as €1.4975 per one pound sterling.

The direct quotation method is used in most countries for dealings between banks and their customers. The indirect quotation method is used in the US for the dollar and in the UK for sterling. In foreign exchange dealings between banks, it is usual to quote the value of currencies against the dollar, in terms of units of currency per dollar, i.e. using the indirect quotation method for the dollar.

An exception is the sterling/dollar rate, known as cable, that is quoted in the markets in terms of dollars per pound.

Following the arrival of the euro in 1999, it has become established practise to quote prices for the euro against other currencies using the euro as the base currency.

Cross Rates

Although banks deal with non-bank customers in any convertible currency, for example sterling/Hong Kong dollars, Swiss francs/Greek drachmas, and so on, the inter-bank market normally quotes currencies against the dollar. This avoids the trouble of having to quote many individual rates between currencies. The exchange rate for any non-dollar currencies is then calculated from their respective dollar exchange rates, to derive a cross rate. For example the Swiss franc/Hong Kong dollar exchange rate can be derived from the dollar/Swiss franc and the dollar/ Hong Kong dollar rates.

Exchange cross rates are rates between two currencies where neither one is the dollar. A table of cross rates, is shown opposite. This includes exchange rates against the dollar. Rates in this table are the mid prices between the bid and offer.

This illustrates, for example, that at the close of the London market on May 17, the exchange rates between the Swiss franc and sterling were £0.4111 per SFr1 and SFr2.431 per £1. Yen are shown in multiples of 100, and so at closing prices on May 17, cross rates were ¥199.5 per £1 and £0.00501 per ¥1.

The sterling/Canadian dollar cross rate, for example, 2.3711, is the inverse of the Canadian dollar/sterling cross rate, 0.42174.

Note: the Canadian dollar/sterling rate is the number of pounds sterling to one Canadian dollar with the Canadian dollar as the base currency, and the sterling/Canadian dollar rate is the number of Canadian dollars to one pound sterling with sterling as the base currency.

Exchange Cross Rates

May 17		DKr	NKr	SKr	SFr	£	C$	$	¥	€
Denmark	(DKr)	10	11.03	12.09	2.155	0.886	2.096	1.436	176.8	1.345
Norway	(NKr)	9.064	10	10.96	1.953	0.803	1.900	1.302	160.3	1.219
Sweden	(SKr)	8.272	9.126	10	1.783	0.733	1.734	1.188	146.3	1.113
Switzerland	(SFr)	4.640	5.120	5.610	1	0.411	0.973	0.666	82.06	0.624
UK	(£)	11.28	12.45	13.64	2.431	1	2.365	1.620	199.5	1.517
Canada	(C$)	4.771	5.264	5.768	1.028	0.423	1	0.685	84.37	0.642
US	($)	6.964	7.684	8.419	1.501	0.617	1.460	1	123.2	0.937
Japan	(¥)	5.655	6.239	6.836	1.219	0.501	1.185	0.812	100	0.761
Euro	(€)	7.434	8.202	8.987	1.602	0.659	1.558	1.068	131.5	1

Danish krona, Norwegian krona and Swedish krona per 10; Yen per 100

Example

Suppose we have the following spot rates against the dollar.

Dollar/Danish krona ($/DKr)	6.9631-6.9651
Dollar/Swiss franc ($/SFr)	1.5005-1.5008

(These are the spot rates against the dollar to which the table of cross rates applies. The letters in brackets, $, DKr and SFr are three-letter identity codes used by FX dealers for traded currencies, in this example the dollar, Danish krona and Swiss franc respectively. These identity codes are called Swift codes, because they were devised by Swift, the Society for Worldwide Interbank Financial Telecommunications.)

Analysis

The DKr/SFr cross rate, i.e. the cross rate for the Danish krona against the Swiss franc, can be calculated from these rates.

For a company to sell Swiss francs in exchange for Danish krona at the spot rate, a bank will quote a price of

1.5005 = rate for bank to sell Swiss francs for dollars
6.9651 = rate for bank to buy dollars for krona

= SFr0.2154 per DKr1, or SFr2.154 per DKr10

Similarly, for a company to buy Swiss francs in exchange for krona, a bank will quote a price of

<u>1.5008</u> = rate for bank to buy Swiss francs for dollars
6.9631 = rate for bank to sell dollars for krona

= SFr0.2155 per DKr1, or SFr2.155 per DKr10

Most inter-bank FX transactions do not involve cross rates, i.e. do not involve the exchange of two non-dollar currencies. A bank wishing to buy yen and sell Swiss francs would sell Swiss francs for dollars and buy yen with the dollars. However, some major cross rates increasingly are traded by banks in addition to dollar-based rates. As the euro becomes more established, it is likely that a large number of FX transactions will involve buying or selling euros in exchange for other non-dollar currencies.

Where cross-rates are traded by banks it is unnecessary for FX traders to calculate the exchange rates from two dollar rates, although smaller banks will still unwind positions using two dollar trades, as illustrated in the previous example.

Volatility of Spot Exchange Rates

The spot exchange rates in major currencies such as dollar/yen, euro/dollar, and sterling/dollar have become increasingly volatile as the volume of foreign exchange transactions has increased.

In the early days of the FX market, transactions were purely trade- or investment-related, and there was little dealing between banks operating in FX markets.

A bank that transacted a spot deal with a company, and bought sterling for dollars for example, would have the exposure until a matching transaction, in which it bought dollars and sold sterling, squared its position. Now a bank can eliminate its exposure instantly with another bank and lock in a profit of one or two points. A profit of two points on buying and selling £100 million against dollars would be $20,000, (£100 million x $0.02 per £1) for example.

In addition to these ripple effects from a trade-related transaction that can create transaction volume several times the original amount, there are speculative transactions. These are outright gambles on future exchange rate movements, conducted by bank dealers, investment managers, brokers or, less often, by companies. If they think a currency is about to rise in value they buy it, anticipating a subsequent sale at a profit. If the currency is expected to fall, they will sell it short, i.e. sell currency they do not have, in anticipation of buying it back, at a lower rate, in order to generate a profit.

To put such activity into perspective, estimates of speculative FX trading and inter-bank FX trading vary between 90% and 98% of total foreign exchange turnover. Only 2-10% of turnover is derived from trade transactions and capital investment flows. In view of this large volume of speculative and inter-bank trading, it is perhaps not surprising that exchange rates are so volatile. Such trading is primarily short term and is rarely driven by considered views on the appropriate level of a currency. It also generates a considerable degree of white noise, where a spot exchange rate fluctuates during the trading day, often to settle at the close of day near its opening level.

The problem for non-bank corporates, buying or selling currency for their own trading or investment purposes, is that the exchange rate for their own transactions will be influenced by the uncertainties and volatility created by speculative dealing activity.

This can distort the value of a currency and consequently put the profits of non-bank trading companies at risk from an adverse exchange rate movement, caused by large inter-bank transactions.

Liquidity

The market for a currency is said to be liquid when customers can buy or sell readily any quantity of the currency. A feature of liquid markets is competition between banks resulting in narrow spreads between bid and offered prices. Liquidity in most currencies varies from one FX center to another, and between the spot and forward markets. For example, there is a liquid spot market for the Canadian dollar in Toronto, New York and London, but in other centers, the Canadian dollar market is much less liquid, and customers have more difficulty in finding a bank willing to buy or sell the currency at a competitive price.

The liquidity in the London market is reflected in the dealing bid-offer spreads that tend to be narrower than those of other major markets.

Narrower London spreads lead to the routing of more business to the London market. To stem this flow, quotes in the US markets tend to match the narrower spreads available in London when the time zones overlap and the two markets are open simultaneously. However, when the London market closes at 4.30pm there tends to be an immediate widening of spreads in the US market.

Interbank trading in currencies does have one significant benefit for trade-related and investment-related FX transactions. The high volume of speculative interbank trading creates much greater liquidity in the market that narrows the bid-offer spreads. This offsets, to some extent, the problems of volatility in exchange rates created by speculative interbank trading.

4

Making a Spot Transaction

Spot transactions are initiated by a request to a bank to buy or sell a specified quantity of one currency in exchange for another. Banks deal directly with each other. One bank's dealing room will telephone another to check a rate it is quoting, and perhaps to make a transaction. A large non-bank corporate might use any one of several banks with which it has regular FX dealings, in the expectation that the banks will try to offer keener prices to secure a transaction with the company. Smaller companies normally will approach the bank that handles all or most of their banking arrangements.

Bid-offer Spreads

A company wishing to make a spot foreign currency transaction will be quoted a price that is either the market spot rate for large transactions, or a rate based on the interbank spot rate, but more favorable to the bank, for smaller transactions. On small deals, the size of the spread offered by a bank will be much greater than for substantial deals. A large corporate with its own treasury dealing room will be offered superior spreads, much as shown in the financial press. The rate offered will be intended to compensate the bank for the fixed administrative cost involved in the foreign exchange transaction.

Banks can offer narrow spreads to other banks and to very large corporates on the basis that a small profit percentage on a large volume transaction can produce a satisfactory total profit. Only large companies with very high credit ratings are likely to receive a narrow spread comparable with price quotes for interbank deals.

Example

Bank Omega makes two deals in the interbank market, when the dollar/ Mexican peso spot rate is 9.4650-9.4750

Deal 1. It buys $10 million, selling Mexican pesos at 9.4650
Deal 2. It sells $10 million, buying Mexican pesos at 9.4750

	In	Out
Deal 1	$10,000,000	Peso94,650,000
Deal 2	Peso94,750,000	$10,000,000
Net result		

	Peso
In	94,750,000
Out	94,650,000
Profit	100,000

The dollars sold and bought net out, leaving the bank with a profit of Peso100,000 for transactions of $10 million based on a spread of 100 points between bid and offer rates.

A bank's FX dealers might quote different rates for the dollar against sterling in the following bands

Up to $5,000	Widest spread
$5,000-$100,000	Narrower spread for larger transactions
$100,000-$2,000,000	Narrower spread for larger transactions
$2,000,000-$50,000,000	Spot rate, narrowest spread
Over $50,000,000	Wider spread reflecting the currency risk of such a large deal

A major non-bank company, buying or selling dollars in batches of $5 million against sterling would be quoted a spread of 10 points maximum, e.g. $1.6200-1.6210. In contrast, a local bank might quote a spread of 900 points, i.e. nine cents, to tourists buying or selling $500 at a time, e.g. $1.5550-1.6450.

Even a large company will encounter wider spreads in spot rates for nonmajor currencies. A large corporate purchase of Venezuelan bolivars would produce a spread as high as 2-3%, and perhaps 5% or more for smaller transactions, despite the significant amount of currency involved. This wider spread for thinly traded currencies reflects dealing banks' perceptions of the risks and their own hedging costs inherent in such transactions.

Before making a currency transaction, a small company should check a recently published exchange rate, for example, the previous day's closing prices in the financial press, noting both the rates and the spread. A selling and buying rate then can be obtained by telephone from the bank. The rate almost certainly will have changed since the previous day's close, but the size of the spread will give some indication of the transaction cost.

The company should avoid indicating whether it intends to buy or sell. If the bank knows the company's intentions, it might offer a narrow spread but move the bid and offer prices to the company's disadvantage.

Organization of FX Dealing within Banks

In a large clearing bank that deals extensively in foreign currencies, the organization for FX operations will be based on a hierarchy. The senior management of the bank's treasury operation fix in broad terms the currencies they will trade, a decision based on trading resources, expertise, available capital and the profit potential of particular currencies.

The bank will have a central FX dealing room in each country where it operates. For example, ABC Bank of the US might have dealing rooms in Tokyo, Sydney, Singapore, London, New York and other centers. New York might be the main center, but currency traders within each center will keep in contact with each other in order to co-ordinate the bank's worldwide trading operations.

Increasing use of sophisticated technology, plus increasing competition for business between banks, is leading to some rationalization. Many banks now have just one major center in each time zone.

Dealing Strategy and Tactics
A bank's foreign exchange department will review its dealing strategy each day before the markets open, and decide its tactics for the day in each currency. Dealing strategy is influenced by the bank's expectations of future currency movements over the next few days, weeks or months.

The daily early-morning assessment will take into consideration

- closing rates in other FX markets. In London for example, a bank will look at closing rates in New York for the previous day and at closing rates in the major dealing centers of the far east
- new economic or political developments
- the bank's own foreign exchange position in each currency.

The outcome of the early-morning meeting should be to plan any modifications to the bank's currency positions.

Long and Short Positions in a Currency

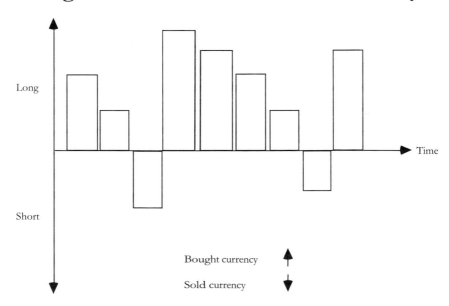

A bank that trades actively in the FX markets has to maintain currency bank accounts, known as nostro accounts, in all the currencies in which it trades to meet payment requirements as they fall due. Current accounts therefore are maintained with correspondent banks in other countries. For example, a US bank will keep a UK sterling current account with a UK correspondent bank, a Swiss franc current account with a Swiss correspondent bank, a Hong Kong dollar account with a correspondent in Hong Kong, and so on.

A bank's trading desk is long in a currency where the total open position – that is current balance forward dates: minus money payable at forward dates – is positive, and is short in a currency where the total open position is negative.

A bank's position in any currency is continually changing, as the currency is bought or sold in daily trading transactions, although new FX market transactions can be made to maintain its required position. Buying a currency lengthens the bank's position in that currency, selling a currency shortens the position.

A bank's position in each currency has to be managed. There are two elements to managing a currency position

- the total net figure for amounts to be received and paid in the currency, and
- the value dates, i.e. the timing, of all such payments.

Dealing Activity
Within each FX center, a bank will have a specialist spot market trader for each currency in which it deals. For example, ABC Bank in New York will have a spot trader for dollars against sterling, another for deutschemarks and another for yen. The trader keeps a book of the purchases and sales of the currency transacted on behalf of the bank. If the aim is to keep a square position, buying and selling equal quantities of the currency, the trader will adjust bid and offered spot prices according to demand and supply from customers.

For example, suppose a German bank is quoting 1.0365-1.0375 for the euro/dollar rate, and wishes to maintain its current position in dollars. If it then transacts a deal involving the sale of $5million in exchange for euros, it will want to buy dollars to restore its position. It could therefore alter its quoted rates to 1.0362-1.0372, i.e. raise the value of the dollar against the euro (lower the value of the euro against the dollar), hoping that its new rate will attract sellers of dollars. However, the market is very competitive, and banks must avoid the risk of setting rates that are significantly out of line with other banks.

The job of the spot market trader is to set the bank's spot prices. When a call is received from a customer asking for a quotation, the call is handled by an intermediary in the bank's dealing room who will ask for a spot price quotation from the trader in the currency. If the transaction is agreed, the trader is informed, so that he can keep his book up to date.

Banks aim to make their profit on the spread between their buying and selling rates from commercial transactions. They also try to earn speculative profits on favorable exchange rate movements.

- If a dealer buys a currency, he/she normally will look to lay off the purchase, selling the currency to another bank or corporate buyer.
- Spot prices vary according to supply and demand in the market, so if a dealer wants to lay off a deal to earn a profit, speed is essential. Therefore dealers commonly will sell currency immediately after buying it, and vice versa.

Speed is critical when deciding which rate to offer.

- If the bank is long in the currency, the dealer will offer a spot rate more attractive to a buyer of that currency than a seller, i.e. he/she will lower the rate.
- If the bank is short in the currency, it will be eager to buy, and will offer higher spot rates.
- If the bank already has a square position, the rate being offered will depend on the dealer's view of how easily and quickly he/she can lay off a deal.

FX Dealing Structure in a Large Retail Bank

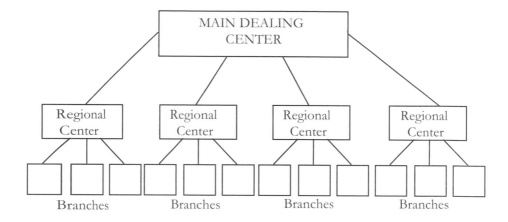

Large banks may have a network of regional FX dealing centers, where smaller orders are transacted. Information about the bank's spot prices will be fed through to the regional center from the bank's main dealing room. Orders into the regional center will be received either directly from customers or via local branches of the bank.

In a large clearing bank, the local branches are important points of first contact for many customers, and in any sizeable branch there will be an official who specializes in foreign exchange.

Many banks do not have a branch network. They will operate with just a central dealing room, handling only large transactions, and often specializing in particular currencies.

Dealing Relationships

Good relationships between bank dealers and their customers, such as other banks and corporate treasury dealers, are vital in a system where deals are done rapidly and transactions are executed orally. It is also essential for good communication between dealers within the bank and the account officer responsible for setting and monitoring credit limits.

For example, a bank's dealer will want to be certain that a corporate customer has sufficient credit lines from the bank and that he/she is dealing with an authorized representative.

In currency trading between a bank and a corporate customer, agreements are made initially by telephone, and later confirmed in writing. This requires a degree of trust between the parties.

Procedures for currency trading depend on

- the regularity of the company's FX transactions with the bank, and
- the size of the transactions.

A company will arrange its FX transactions with its local branch, a regional dealing center of the bank that employs currency and trade specialists, or the bank's main FX center for direct contact with the main currency trader.

For purposes of currency trading, there are three distinct categories of company.

- Small companies that conduct their FX transactions through their bank's local branch.
- Larger companies that have more extensive foreign trading interests, and are encouraged to contact the FX dealing center of their bank, and might consider other banks for large transactions.
- Other banks, and multinationals with an FX dealing room in their treasury department, with direct telephone access to the dealing rooms of major banks, and screen-based market information.

Large corporate dealing rooms operate in different ways. Some are profit centers, and provide banking services in foreign exchange to subsidiaries or business units in the group. They will deal in the FX markets also and so supply a link between the FX markets and the rest of the group. Some dealing rooms are encouraged to make speculative profits from short-term transactions in the FX markets, while others are not.

Examples

The following assumes a good business relationship between a company and its bank. Without a good relationship, the bank might refuse to make a transaction, fearing perhaps that the customer might be a bad credit risk.

Infrequent Deals in Small Transactions

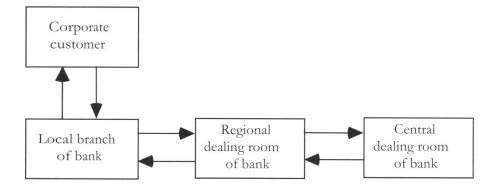

The company phones its local branch and asks to make an FX transaction. The branch official takes the details and phones the bank's international division FX dealer. The FX dealer has access to dealing rates on a screen, and quotes the appropriate exchange rate. The branch official phones this rate to the customer, who is given a deal number.

The company is then asked to confirm in writing the request to buy or sell the currency. The local branch is authorized to make any necessary payments out of the company's account. The bank sends a contract note to the company, whose account is credited or debited on the value date, that will be two working days later for a spot transaction.

Sometimes this procedure is shortened and the branch official will not phone for approval before making the transaction on the company's behalf. The obvious disadvantage of this approach is that the company has insufficient control over the exchange rate at which the transaction is executed. In addition, the bank dealing room has a captive customer, and no incentive to quote a competitive rate. Not surprisingly, rates quoted through this route tend to be less competitive than those available from dealing directly with the bank's dealing room.

More Frequent Deals, still in Small Transactions

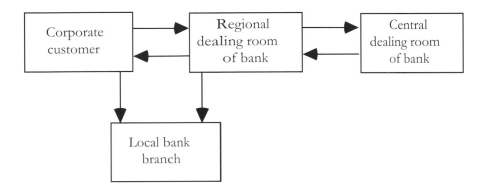

The company is given a phone number for calling directly an FX dealer at the bank's international division. In this case transactions are agreed directly between the FX dealer and the company. The company is then asked to confirm all transactions in writing and the bank sends a contract note for each transaction.

The local branch of the bank is informed of the details for payments into/from the company's account by the bank's dealer while the company also arranges for payments with the local branch.

Frequent Deals, in Large Transactions

In this scenario the company is likely to have at least one specialist dealer in FX in its treasury department. Medium and large companies with a regular flow of foreign currency transactions can access the trading room of major banks by direct phone link. For major players, the bank

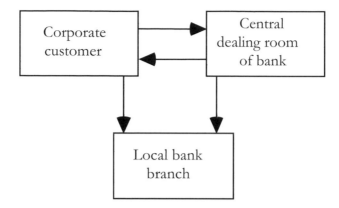

pays for direct phone lines, exclusive to the company and bank. These companies have several dealers who execute business transactions at the most economical rate for the company. In medium-sized companies, the responsibility for treasury dealing often is combined with other financial management duties.

When a company dealer telephones the dealing room, the call usually will be answered by the bank's corporate dealers. Their role is to connect the corporate clients and the bank traders who run the various currency books because the traders have to concentrate on managing the book, and do not have time to talk to companies direct.

NATIONAL DYNAMICS
PUBLIC LIMITED COMPANY

Company Headquarters
Electron House
North West Bank   Blenheim Palace Road
Finsbury Circus   Reading
London   Berkshire
EC2   RG7 6QQ
                            Telephone: (0734) 154826
Your reference: ND/NW   Our reference:
Your deal no: 0001   Our deal no: FRG63318A
                            Date: 4 Jan 2000

Dear Sirs

We confirm having sold to you US DOLLAR 7,000,000.00 having purchased
from you POUND STERLING 4,228,840.69 at the rate: 1.6553 for value date:
6 Jan 2000.

Please pay POUND STERLING 4,228,840.69
for value date   6 Jan 2000
to   Alpha Bank plc
                                  City Office
                                  Lombard Street
                                  London
                                  EC3

for our account   National Dynamics
account number   9999999
bank sort code   99-99-99

We will pay US DOLLAR 7,000,000.00

for value date   6 Jan 2000
                                  NorthWest Bank
                                   New York
                                   US
to your account   NorthWest Bank London

Yours faithfully

Authorized signatory   Authorized signatory

One of the bank's corporate dealers establishes the company's needs in terms of the currency and amount to be dealt, and checks that the bank has allocated a credit limit to that company to accept it as a counterparty. The bank dealer then obtains a price quote from the trader and passes it back to the company treasury dealer for acceptance or rejection. The volatility of the spot markets is such that spot rates are valid only for a matter of seconds. If the company dealer considers the price reasonable, he or she gives verbal acceptance and then repeats the terms of the transaction.

Foreign currency transactions are agreed between the company and the bank that gives a competitive price. It is not possible to shop around widely for the lowest price because the constantly changing spot rate prevents pricing comparisons.

Ideally, the FX dealer at a company would obtain at least two simultaneous quotes for a spot transaction. However, in practise this is rare, even with two dealers working together. The communications link between company dealer-bank corporate dealer-bank trader and back can take ten to 90 seconds to obtain a spot quote, even on direct dealing lines. Quotes are valid for only a few seconds, and it is rare for them to arrive simultaneously. A more reliable comparison is to check the best price for that FX rate quoted on a real-time basis on screen. An experienced dealer also will be aware of what a price-efficient spread between bid and offer rates in that particular currency should be.

Execution Fees
Banks sometimes demand execution fees for arranging currency sales or purchases for small companies, and these can be substantial in relation to the size of a minor transaction. Large companies normally do not pay such fees.

Documentation and Contractual Obligations

FX transactions are made by phone. In the main dealing center of a bank, transactions are recorded on a deal ticket. The deal ticket simply will record details of the counterparty, the amount sold or purchased, the exchange rate, the settlement date, the proceeds and bank payment details. The ticket may be physical. Increasingly, however, dealers enter their trades directly into a computerized dealing system.

Deal Ticket

ALPHA BANK PLC, LONDON

Sold to	Omega Bank, Amsterdam
Amount	$2,500,000
Rate	1.5010
Value	June 15 2000
To be paid to	Their account with Statcorp Bank, New York
Proceeds	£1,665,556.30
To be paid from	Their account with Alpha Bank

The bank will issue a confirmation listing the details of the spot trade that should arrive the next day, i.e. one day before settlement. In return, the bank will expect a letter confirming details from the customer, if it is dealing direct. A sample letter of a confirmation from a corporate customer is shown on page 43.

Dollar Spot Rates: Reuters' Screen Information

Reference code for Reuters' page on which the quote is carried

Most recent €/$ spot rate quote in the FX market at the moment

Day's low quote for $/SFr rate

Reuters' page code

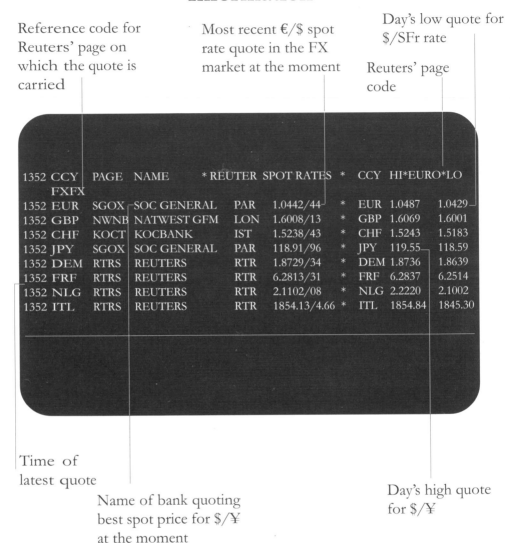

1352 CCY	PAGE	NAME	* REUTER	SPOT RATES	*	CCY	HI*EURO*LO	
FXFX								
1352 EUR	SGOX	SOC GENERAL	PAR	1.0442/44	*	EUR	1.0487	1.0429
1352 GBP	NWNB	NATWEST GFM	LON	1.6008/13	*	GBP	1.6069	1.6001
1352 CHF	KOCT	KOCBANK	IST	1.5238/43	*	CHF	1.5243	1.5183
1352 JPY	SGOX	SOC GENERAL	PAR	118.91/96	*	JPY	119.55	118.59
1352 DEM	RTRS	REUTERS	RTR	1.8729/34	*	DEM	1.8736	1.8639
1352 FRF	RTRS	REUTERS	RTR	6.2813/31	*	FRF	6.2837	6.2514
1352 NLG	RTRS	REUTERS	RTR	2.1102/08	*	NLG	2.2220	2.1002
1352 ITL	RTRS	REUTERS	RTR	1854.13/4.66	*	ITL	1854.84	1845.30

Time of latest quote

Name of bank quoting best spot price for $/¥ at the moment

Day's high quote for $/¥

The main part of the screen shows spot rates for the dollar against other major currencies. As the currency (CCY) column indicates, there are spot rates shown for: €/$, £/$, $/SFr, $/Y and $ against the four legacy currencies, the deutschemark, franc, guilder and lira.

The screen is divided into two halves. The left-hand side shows the best spot prices currently being quoted for each currency against the dollar, and the bank that is offering these prices. The right-hand side shows the day's high and low prices.

Because a spot trade is settled two business days after execution, it is important to dispatch the confirmation letter on the day of transaction so that any mistakes can be identified before settlement.

Small companies dealing through their branch might be asked to provide written confirmation of their requirements before the trade is executed, so subsequent confirmation is unnecessary. The exchange of bank account details will then form part of prior notification.

Companies should be aware that the bank(s) with which they deal would want to control or avoid the currency risks to which they, in turn, are exposed. This means that usually they will want to maintain a square position in each foreign currency, with assets matching liabilities.

If a company buys dollars from a UK bank, the bank's holdings of dollars will fall, and the bank therefore might enter the FX markets to buy more dollars to keep its position square.

Obviously, a bank will aggregate its individual transactions with customers, and will enter the FX markets to buy or sell substantial quantities of currency in interbank deals. Even so, the principle of trying to keep a square position is valid.

In order to manage its currency exposures in this way, a spot FX transaction, once made, is binding on both parties.

Settlement

Spot transactions are settled two working days after the deal is made, the two payments being made simultaneously. For example, a dollar/ Canadian dollar transaction would be settled through the international banking system, by a transfer of Canadian dollars (in Canada) and a transfer of dollars (in the US) on the same day.

Because of the nature of the clearing systems in most countries, it is not until one day later that each party to an FX transaction can find out whether the payment due from the other party has been received. As a consequence, each party to a foreign exchange transaction runs a credit risk.

To keep credit risk within limits, banks usually will agree to transact large amounts with prime names only, i.e. organizations with a top credit rating. The size of transactions will be limited for lesser names.

The five or six-hour time difference between New York and Europe can add to the problem. A large proportion of FX transactions involves the dollar on one side, and a payment in dollars can be initiated five or six hours later than a payment in a European currency.

For example, suppose that a spot sterling/dollar trade is agreed on May 20, for settlement on May 22. On May 22, one of the counterparties to the trade will have to settle in sterling in the UK. The other counterparty will settle in dollars in the US, but can wait up to five hours later. During this time, confirmation can be cabled to the US, if requested, that the sterling payment has been made, but the same information is not available to the counterparty receiving payment in dollars.

Tracking Spot Exchange Rates

The major cost in FX dealing for a large corporate is the failure to obtain a good spot rate quote for its trades, and so tracking spot exchange rates is a significant element in the dealer's job.

The volatility of spot exchange rates means that they are continually adjusted by the banks that make markets in them. The most effective way for a large corporate dealer to track the constantly changing rate is through one of the real-time information services, such as Reuters. Each system has composite pages displaying the most recent spot rates in each major exchange rate at any time in the day.

This data is adapted by the bank's own software for the dealers' screens; but usually, for both bank dealers and corporate treasurers of larger companies, it comprises the following

- current rates available from each bank
- details of recent deals
- a news service, i.e. for information about political events, or economic statistics, as they are announced.

A bank's dealer also needs to monitor his own book constantly, and will have an in-house computer system that indicates the deals he has made and at which rates.

Spot prices on an FX page on a real-time information services screen continually adjust in hectic trading conditions, sometimes every few seconds, as trading creates fluctuations in exchange rates.

The cost of such services is prohibitive for a company transacting only a few, low-value FX trades per year but not for major corporate dealing rooms, and the dealing rooms of banks, where cross rates will be available instantly on information screens. Clearly, a company must believe that the information supplied is of sufficient value to justify such a cost.

There are other ways for companies with smaller FX exposures to monitor spot rates, albeit on a less accurate basis. The financial newspapers publish exchange rates for the main trading currencies against other major currencies daily. They show the closing bid-offer rates and the daily trading range. As a result, small companies can at least verify the rate that their bank has achieved for them relative to the intra-day fluctuations in the particular spot rate, and its closing rate.

Technology for FX Dealing

Foreign exchange dealing by banks and large non-bank corporates relies on continuously up-dated information, relayed to each dealer by a computer screen.

Traditionally market data has been supplied in video format by sources such as Reuters. The subscriber bank or company pays for the service, and without further processing, the exchange rate data appears on the screen in a fixed format.

Since the 1980s, most dealers have taken market data from information providers in digital feeds. These allow in-house computer systems to process the data and transform it to suit the dealer's own particular requirements. Therefore the market data is presented on dealers' screens in a customized format, perhaps using graphics.

Individual dealers might have their own workstations with PCs using software packages to process market data from the information providers. Alternatively, incoming market data might be processed immediately by a mainframe computer before being transmitted to dealers' screens.

5

Practical Guidelines for Spot Transactions

A customer initiates a foreign exchange transaction by calling a bank, and the bank will respond by quoting a price. The customer might be another bank or a non-bank corporate. To obtain a satisfactory rate of exchange and to avoid mistakes, customers should follow a number of practical guidelines relating to the timing of the transaction, pre-dealing preparation and the price (exchange rate) at which the deal is made.

These guidelines vary according to whether the customer is a large corporate with its own dealing room, or small and involved in just a few FX transactions, or for smaller amounts.

Timing the Transaction

The customer in an FX transaction normally will have some latitude in choosing when to deal, or enter the market.

Price Volatility
Entering the market should be avoided when it is particularly volatile such as when an important economic indicator like the consumer price index is about to be published, or when a major news item has been announced but not yet evaluated. At such times banks widen their spreads, sometimes dramatically, to protect their position. Until the indicator is announced or the news digested there will be uncertainty about what the new market level for the exchange rate will be. By widening their spreads temporarily, banks protect themselves against movements, up or down, in currency prices.

Price Efficiency

Banks dealing in currencies will quote prices of their own choosing. At any time, the prices of some banks will be more favorable to the customer than those of other banks. For example, one bank might quote a sterling/dollar rate of 1.5810-1.5815, another a rate of 1.5800-1.5805, another a rate of 1.5820-1.5830 and so on. Other banks and large non-bank corporates who wish to buy or sell currencies should try to deal with banks that offer the keenest prices. Because prices are continually changing, this is not such an easy task as it might appear. However, some banks deal extensively in one, a few, or most currencies, and these major players are most likely to give the best rates. Other banks will quote wider spreads to make their profit from buying and re-selling.

Large organizations that can make FX transactions in different financial centers around the world at any time of day should deal at times when prices are most competitive and banks are offering the narrowest spreads. This is commonly during the trading hours of the London FX markets.

Preparing to Deal (Large Dealing Room)

Spot transactions are settled quickly by phone and so a dealer must be sure, before picking up the phone, which bank to approach, what an acceptable price level will be, and which of the two quoted prices (bid or offer rate) will be the appropriate one for the planned transaction.

- *Selecting a bank.* The dealer should decide which bank or banks to invite to quote for a transaction. Many banks provide competitive spot quotes although the actual choice might be influenced by relationship considerations. A company could allocate its spot business to a bank providing a scarcer, and so valuable, banking resource, such as loan finance. There are several hundred banks in London that deal in FX, but many specialize by currency; some might prefer to deal in Asian currencies, Swedish krona or Canadian dollars. A dealer therefore might establish a dealing relationship with those specialist banks for particular currencies.

● *Establishing acceptable prices.* Before starting to deal, each dealer should be told the precise price levels or the latitude (a range of prices) for the trading currencies that must be achieved. The dealer must then work within these parameters because there will be no time to check spot prices with management once dealing has begun. For example, a dealer responsible for trading sterling/dollars may be given a trading range for the bid rate and a trading range for the offer rate. If a bank quotes a price outside this range, the dealer will phone another bank.

Before seeking quotes on exchange rates, it is advisable to calculate the approximate cost in domestic currency of each planned transaction. This will indicate the consequences of each extra point that the dealer can obtain from the bank. For a $3 million transaction, when the exchange rate is around the £1 = $1.50 level, each one point of price ($0.0001) is worth about £133 – a considerable amount.

● *Bid and offer rates.* When inviting a bank to quote for a spot transaction, the dealer should at first specify the currency and the amount, but not whether it is a buy or sell transaction. For example, a dealer might ask a bank to quote spot prices for $5 million against sterling. The bank will then quote bid and offer rates. Only if the quoted prices are acceptable will the dealer then specify the direction of transaction. So it is important to know which of the two rates is appropriate for the planned transaction, because the bank will expect an immediate acceptance or rejection of the quote.

Dealers often will refer to dealing sides, meaning the bid and offer rates. For example, if the spot rate for euros/Canadian dollars is 1.5475-1.5478, a customer buying Canadian dollars (C$) will be dealing on the left-hand side of the spread at C$1.5475 to one euro, and a customer selling C$ for euros will be dealing on the right-hand side of the spread at 1.5478. The general rule is that the customer deals at the less advantageous price, and the bank deals at the more advantageous price.

A dealer should determine whether a transaction would be at the left- or right-hand side of the quoted spread

- first, to ensure that the price quoted by the bank is valid and acceptable, and
- second, to avoid disputes with the bank about the rate, or who was the buyer and who was the seller in the transaction.

Preparing to Deal (Small Company)

Even in small companies, preparing carefully for an FX transaction might achieve a better rate from the bank. The finance director or financial controller who is making the transaction should

- check the previous day's closing prices for the exchange rate in the financial press and note the size of the spread between the bid and offer rates. Contact the bank and ask the prices that it would likely offer for a given spot transaction. The spread offered by the bank will be wider than in the financial press, but if it seems too wide, it should be challenged. The bank either will have to justify its prices or offer a narrower spread
- ask the branch to put him/her directly in touch with the bank's dealing room for larger transactions of around $300,000 upwards to avoid having to arrange the transaction with the branch as broker. The company then can ask the dealing room to quote prices, and benefit from the narrower spreads normally available for direct dealings and larger transactions.

Pricing

There are several ways a company can obtain continually competitive price quotations from its banks. Demanding efficient prices should be a prime task of regular dealers in FX, because savings in the long term can be enormous.

In a large company with its own dealing room, two immediate price checks can be made when a spot FX quote is received

- the size of the bid/offer spread, and
- whether or not the spread is biased within the general market level quoted on the price information screen.

If the screen is showing a dollar/Hong Kong dollar rate of HK$7.7530-7.7550, for example, then the spread is 20 points. A quote from a bank on a tighter spread of ten points should fall broadly in the center of this range at HK$7.7535-7.7545 in a stable market. If it does not and is quoted at HK$7.7532-7.7542, there will be a bias towards the lower end of the spread on the dealing screen. In a moving market this will be less obvious, and screen prices may differ considerably from the real market. However, if a bank wants the customer to sell Hong Kong dollars rather than buy them, this could be because

- the bank trader has a mismatched book, sales of HK$ exceeding purchases, and is trying to generate transactions to square the position by improving the price on one side of the transaction, in this example by encouraging customers to sell that currency
- the market is moving in one direction and the price movement — in this example downwards — has not yet been reflected in the screen price
- the bank trader thinks that he knows which side the customer is dealing on and is trying to squeeze an extra point or two on the price to improve the bank's profit on the deal.

This last point is common when it is known that a company's dealings are largely in one direction; for example, if a customer is a major non-US corporate who is known to be a major recipient of dollars. To prevent the bank moving the spread in this way, the customer can complain to its account officer at the bank and perhaps even stop dealing with the bank.

Alternatively, the company, every so often, might deal in the unexpected direction, buying a currency instead of selling it as normal, or vice versa. Hence a non-US company that is a major recipient of dollars, and so normally wants to sell dollars, will sometimes buy dollars and exacerbate its currency exposure just to sharpen up future bank quotes. While it may cost the company in the short run, the net benefit from greater price efficiency far outweighs any such cost for a company dealing regularly and in large amounts of FX.

A dealer should insist on reading back the details of an agreed transaction to the bank counterparty, always confirming the settlement amount as this cross-checks the direction (buying or selling), rate, and principal amount of the transaction within a single figure. If, for example, £2.5 million have been sold by the customer for euros at €1 = £0.6625, the settlement amount for the company is a euros receipt of €3,773,584.91.

Mistakes can be made in dealing by phone. A company dealer could make a bank dealer believe he is selling currency instead of buying, or vice versa. The amount also could be wrong. If the customer notices an error when sending written confirmation of the deal to the bank, he shouldn't hesitate to admit it. Mistakes are inevitable and honesty in admitting them will preserve a good relationship with the bank.

Over time, a company will be able to determine the price efficiency of a particular bank by keeping a record of all the banks' quoted prices. The company can then talk to each bank on a regular basis to review the competitiveness of its quotes and the number of times its quotes were successful.

It is more difficult for a small company to monitor the price competitiveness of its bank, but if it arranges FX transactions regularly, often it will be worthwhile to keep the bank aware of its concern about prices.

When, after a transaction has been made, the branch notifies the company of the exchange rate obtained and the time the deal was transacted, the company can check the competitiveness of the rate against the market at around that time. This is part of the process of keeping the bank aware of the importance attached to efficient pricing and service on FX transactions. Also it should encourage the bank to secure optimum prices for future transactions.

6

Forward Exchange Contracts

Currency can be traded spot or forward. In the case of a spot transaction, the purchase or sale takes place immediately, for settlement two working days later. In the case of a forward transaction, the purchase or sale is agreed but will take place at some time in the future, thereby fixing the rate for a future exchange of currencies. Forward transactions are known as forward exchange contracts or forward contracts.

Elements of Forward Exchange Contracts

A forward exchange contract, as its name implies, is a contractually binding agreement between two parties, a bank and a non-bank customer, or two banks. Once made, a customer cannot back out of it nor alter its terms, except by arrangement with the contracting bank.

Every forward contract has three main elements, the first two also are features of spot transactions.

- It is a binding agreement to buy or sell a specific quantity of one currency in exchange for another.
- The rate of exchange is fixed when the contract is made. Except in rare instances, this will not be the same as the rate for a spot transaction.
- The contract is for performance, delivery of the currency, at an agreed future time, either a specific date or any time between two specific dates, depending on the contract terms.

Forward Contracts: Features, Benefits and Limitations

Value Dating
The value date of an FX transaction is the date of the actual receipt and payment of the currency.

- For spot transactions, the value date is two working days after the deal date.
- For forward transactions, the value date is measured from the spot value date.

Forward Contracts: Dealing Date and Value Date

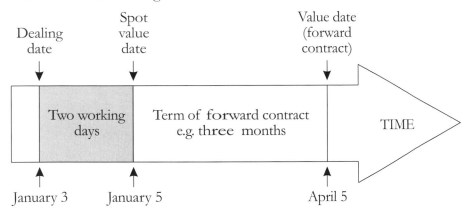

Examples
A three-month forward contract agreed on Tuesday May 12, will have a value date three months after the spot value date (May 14) i.e. August 14.

A one-month forward contract agreed on Monday October 2, will have a value date one month after October 4. This will be November 4. However, November 4 will be a Saturday and not a working day, so the value date moves to Monday November 6.

There is an exception. When the spot value date is the last working day of the current month, the value date for a forward contract will be the last working day of the appropriate month. For example, if the spot value date were Friday March 29, the last working day in March, the following value dates would apply

One month forward contract	Tuesday April 30
Two months' forward contract	Friday May 31
Three months' forward contract	Friday June 28
Six months' forward contract	Monday September 30

This is known as dealing end-end.

Forward Rates and Spot Rates

The forward rate is nearly always higher or lower than the spot rate. Because forward and spot rates differ, one or the other must be more favorable to the customer and less favorable to the bank.

Example 1
Suppose that the sterling/dollar spot rate is £1 = $1.500 and the three-month forward rate is higher, at 1.5150.

A company wishing to buy $1 million would pay £666,666.67 spot and only £660,066.01 at the forward rate. In this situation, it would be cheaper to buy dollars for delivery in three months than for immediate settlement.

On the other hand, a company wishing to sell $1 million at the same rates would receive less for a forward contract arrangement than for a spot sale.

Example 2
Suppose that the euro/Swiss franc rate is €1 = SFr1.5900 spot and lower at SFr1.5800 for a two-month forward contract.

A company wishing to buy SFr1 million would pay €628,930.82 for a spot transaction and €632,911.39, a considerable amount more, for a two-month forward contract.

On the other hand, a company wishing to sell SFr1 million at the same rates would receive fewer euros from a spot sale of the Swiss francs than from a two-month forward sale.

Why Rates Differ

Forward rates are not forecasts of spot exchange rate movements, nor do they reflect the market's expectation of future spot rates. Rather, the difference between a forward exchange rate and the spot rate reflects the interest rate differential between the two currencies.

If forward rates did not reflect interest rate differentials between currencies, investors could use forward contracts to earn a guaranteed profit through arbitrage. Arbitrage is the exploitation of price differences between two financial instruments, or between two financial markets, to make an immediate and certain profit.

Unless spot rates and forward rates reflected the differences in interest rates between two currencies, investors could profit from the price differences between the FX markets and the eurocurrency markets – the money markets for borrowing, depositing, and lending currencies internationally. This important point is explained in the following examples.

Example 1

The interest rate for the Swiss franc is 2% per annum and for the dollar 6% per annum. The dollar/Swiss franc spot exchange rate is $1 = SFr1.50.

An investor with SFr1.5 million and a need for dollars one year hence should be indifferent, financially speaking, as to whether

- the Swiss francs are sold for dollars spot and invested to earn $1,060,000 by the end of the year, or
- the Swiss francs are sold for dollars for value one year hence, and invested until then at 2%, producing SFr1,530,000 (SFr1.5 million plus 2% interest) at the end of the year.

The one-year forward rate should be $1 = 1.4434 (SFr1,530,000 ÷

$1,060,000) to make the investor indifferent about the choice of option. If the one-year forward rate were above or below $1.4434, an investor would earn a bigger income either by

- selling Swiss francs spot for dollars, and investing in dollars, or
- selling Swiss francs forward and investing in Swiss francs.

Market forces of supply and demand should put pressure on the spot rate, forward rate and interest rates until the profiteering opportunities disappear as market prices adjust.

Investor Choices: Swiss Investor with SFr1.5 million

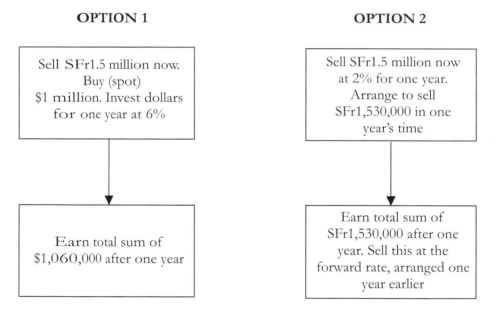

OPTION 1

Sell SFr1.5 million now. Buy (spot) $1 million. Invest dollars for one year at 6%

Earn total sum of $1,060,000 after one year

OPTION 2

Sell SFr1.5 million now at 2% for one year. Arrange to sell SFr1,530,000 in one year's time

Earn total sum of SFr1,530,000 after one year. Sell this at the forward rate, arranged one year earlier

If the forward rate had equaled the spot rate at $1 = SFr1.50, for example, it would have been more profitable to sell the Swiss francs spot and invest in dollars at 6%, to earn $1,060,000 after one year. The alternative option of investing in Swiss francs and selling SFr1.53 million forward would yield only $1,020,000.

Similarly, if the forward rate had been $1 = SFr1.40, investing in Swiss francs at 2% and selling SFr1,530,000 forward would yield about

$1,093,000 that would be more profitable than selling the Swiss francs spot and investing in dollars.

The equilibrium forward rate, as its name implies, leaves the investor no worse or better off. In this example, the equilibrium forward rate is around $1 = SFr1.4434 that generates $1,060,000 whichever option is taken. The one-year forward rate for the Swiss franc against the dollar therefore should be about 0.0566 francs lower than the spot rate, reflecting the interest rate differential and lower Swiss franc interest rates.

Example 2
The interest rate for the euro is 3% and for sterling is 5%. The euro/sterling spot rate is €1 = £0.6600.

The one-year forward rate at which profit-taking opportunities will not exist, is the rate at which a UK investor of £3.3 million is indifferent between

- selling the sterling spot for €5 million and investing for one year at 3%, and
- investing the sterling for one year at 5% and arranging now to sell the proceeds, one year forward.

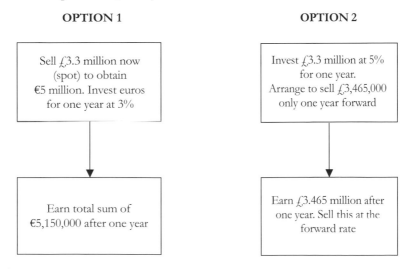

OPTION 1	OPTION 2
Sell £3.3 million now (spot) to obtain €5 million. Invest euros for one year at 3%	Invest £3.3 million at 5% for one year. Arrange to sell £3,465,000 only one year forward
Earn total sum of €5,150,000 after one year	Earn £3.465 million after one year. Sell this at the forward rate

The equilibrium one-year forward rate is about €1 = £0.6728 (£3,465,000 ÷ €5,150,000). This is higher than the spot rate by about

£0.0128, to reflect higher sterling interest rates/lower interest rates for the euro

- if the forward rate is below 0.6728 – €1 = 0.67, it would be more profitable to invest in sterling and sell the £3.465 million forward
- if the forward rate is above 0.6728 – 0.6750 to one euro, it would be more profitable to sell the sterling spot and invest in euros.

The above examples illustrate the key points that

- whether the forward rate is higher or lower than the spot rate depends on which currency yields a higher rate of interest on bank deposits (investments), and
- the difference between spot and forward rates depends on the size of annual interest rate differentials between the two currencies and the term of the forward contract. Differences between spot and forward rates will increase with the term of the forward contract.

Exercise

Interest rates on dollar deposits are 5% per annum and Japanese yen interest rates are 1%. The spot rate is $1 = ¥122.00. Will the forward rate be above or below the spot rate? What will be the one-year forward rate?

Solution

Interest rates are higher on the dollar so the forward rate will be below 122.00.

The one-year forward rate can be estimated as follows. An investor with ¥122 million could sell this currency spot for $1 million and invest the dollars for one year at 5% to earn $1,050,000. Alternatively, the ¥122 million could be invested at 1% for one year to earn ¥123,220,000, and this could be sold forward. The equilibrium forward rate that prevents arbitrage opportunities is about $1 = ¥117.35 (¥123,220,000 ÷ $1,050,000) that is lower than the spot rate.

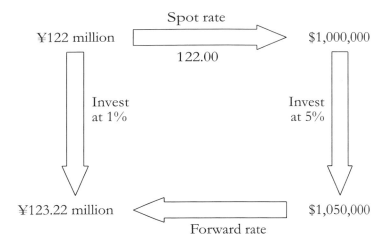

If the two investments are to be equivalent, in one year's time ¥123,220,000 must equal $1,050,000. Hence the forward rate must be

$$\frac{123,220,000}{1,050,000} = 117.35$$

Spot or Forward?

It is easy perhaps to fall into the trap of comparing a spot rate with a forward rate in the belief that there is a *choice* between making a spot or a forward transaction at today's rates. This is not really the case. If a company expects to have a receipt or to make a payment of currency at a date in the future, its choice primarily is between

- making a forward transaction now, at today's rates, for the future date, and
- doing nothing until the future date arrives, and then buying or selling the currency at whatever the spot rate happens to be at that time.

Quoting Forward Rates

Forward rates are quoted in several ways. The most obvious method is to specify the actual rate. Illustrative currency for the euro and the dollar tables are shown on pages 68 and 69.

Euro Spot: Forward against the Euro

May 25		Closing mid point	One month Rate	%PA	Three months Rate	%PA	One year Rate	%PA
Europe								
Czech Rep	(Koruna)	37.9094	38.0581	-4.7	38.3280	-4.4	39.5632	-4.4
Denmark	(DKr)	7.4345	7.4378	-0.5	7.4448	-0.6	7.4805	-0.6
Greece	(Dr)	325.367	327.4357	-7.6	331.0179	-6.9	343.9152	-5.7
Hungary	(Forint)	250.894	253.5488	-12.7	258.7351	-12.5	280.5831	-11.8
Norway	(NKr)	8.2540	8.2860	-4.7	8.3374	-4.0	8.5149	-3.2
Sweden	(SKr)	8.9979	9.0023	-0.6	9.0099	-0.5	9.0542	-0.6
Switzerland	(SFr)	1.5949	1.5926	1.7	1.5884	1.6	1.5720	1.4
UK	(£)	0.6625	0.6640	-2.7	0.6669	-2.7	0.6801	-2.7
Americas								
Canada	(C$)	1.5479	1.5508	-2.2	1.5561	-2.1	1.5828	-2.3
Mexico	(Peso)	10.1034	10.2910	-22.3	10.6351	-21.1	12.3656	-22.4
USA	($)	1.0610	1.0631	-2.4	1.0675	-2.5	1.0902	-2.8
Pacific/Middle East/Africa								
Australia	(A$)	1.6138	1.6170	-2.4	1.6230	-2.3	1.6538	-2.5
Hong Kong	(HK$)	8.2275	8.2456	-2.6	8.2860	-2.8	8.5711	-4.2
Japan	(¥)	130.200	129.9117	2.7	129.3635	2.6	126.8303	2.6
New Zealand	(NZ$)	1.9526	1.9560	-2.1	1.9622	-2.0	1.9963	-2.2
Singapore	(S$)	1.8286	1.8270	1.0	1.8257	0.6	1.8284	0.0
South Africa	(R)	6.6097	6.6809	-12.9	6.8016	-11.6	7.3261	-10.8

Dollar Spot: Forward against the Dollar

May 25		Closing mid point	One month Rate	%PA	Three months Rate	%PA	One year Rate	%PA
Europe								
Denmark	(DKr)	7.1253	7.1131	2.1	7.0884	2.1	6.9673	2.2
Greece	(Dr)	310.515	311.8	-5.0	313.915	-4.4	318.565	-2.6
Norway	(NKr)	7.8650	7.8777	-1.9	7.8928	-1.4	7.8863	-0.3
Sweden	(SKr)	8.5445	8.5305	2.0	8.5014	2.0	8.3595	2.2
Switzerland	(SFr)	1.5263	1.5210	4.2	1.5107	4.1	1.4633	4.1
UK	(£)	1.6037	1.6070	0.3	1.6032	0.1	1.6070	-0.2

Dollar Spot: Forward against the Dollar *(cont)*

May 25		Closing mid point	One month Rate	%PA	Three months Rate	%PA	One year Rate	%PA
Euro	(€)	1.0427	1.0449	-2.5	1.0493	-2.5	1.0723	-2.8
Americas								
Canada	(C$)	1.4708	1.4705	0.2	1.4696	0.3	1.4654	0.4
Mexico	(Peso)	9.4700	9.62	-19.0	9.9	-18.2	11.24	-18.7
Pacific/Middle East/Africa								
Australia	(A$)	1.5171	1.5167	0.3	1.5162	0.2	1.5156	0.1
Hong Kong	(HK$)	7.7570	7.7592	-0.3	7.7645	-0.4	7.8510	-1.2
India	(Rs)	43.0530	43.1975	-4.5	43.5575	-4.9	45.6425	-6.1
Japan	(¥)	120.070	119.55	5.2	118.55	5.1	113.625	5.4
New Zealand	(NZ$)	1.8847	1.8829	1.1	1.8812	0.8	1.8816	0.2
Saudi Arabia	(SR)	3.7505	3.7511	-0.2	3.7545	-0.4	3.776	-0.7
Singapore	(S$)	1.7117	1.7068	3.4	1.6977	3.3	1.6651	2.7
S Africa	(R)	6.0975	6.1465	-9.6	6.228	-8.6	6.545	-7.3
Taiwan	(N$)	32.5775	32.4575	4.4	32.44	1.7	32.4725	0.3
Thailand	(Bt)	39.9650	39.9725	-0.2	36.9875	-0.2	37.265	-0.8

International Currency Interest Rates

May 25	Short term	7 days' notice	One month	Three months	Six months	One year
Euro	$2^9/_{16}$-$2^{15}/_{32}$	$2^{19}/_{32}$-$2^{17}/_{32}$	$2^{19}/_{32}$-$2^{17}/_{32}$	$2^5/_{18}$-$2^1/_2$	$2^{21}/_{32}$-$2^{17}/_{32}$	$2^{11}/_{16}$-$2^5/_8$
Danish Krona	$3^1/_8$ - $2^5/_8$	$3^1/_{16}$ - $2^{29}/_{32}$	$3^3/_{32}$ - $2^{15}/_{16}$	$3^3/_{32}$ - $2^{15}/_{16}$	$3^5/_{32}$ - $2^1/_{32}$	$3^9/_{32}$ - $3^1/_8$
Sterling	5 - $4^7/_8$	$5^9/_{32}$ - $5^3/_{16}$	$5^{11}/_{32}$ - $5^1/_4$	$5^5/_{16}$ - $5^3/_{16}$	$5^1/_4$ - $5^1/_8$	$5^7/_{16}$ - $5^5/_{32}$
Swiss Franc	$1^1/_{16}$ -$^{11}/_{16}$	$1^1/_{32}$ - $^{25}/_{32}$	$^{31}/_{32}$ -$^7/_8$	1 - $^{29}/_{32}$	$1^3/_{32}$ -$^{31}/_{32}$	$1^9/_{32}$ - $1^5/_{32}$
Canadian Dollar	$4^{11}/_{16}$ - $4^9/_{16}$	$4^{11}/_{16}$ - $4^9/_{16}$	$4^{23}/_{32}$ - $4^{19}/_{32}$	$4^{23}/_{32}$ - $4^{19}/_{32}$	$4^3/_4$ - $4^5/_8$	$4^{29}/_{32}$ - $4^{25}/_{32}$
Dollar	$4^{23}/_{32}$ - $4^5/_8$	$4^{29}/_{32}$ - $4^{27}/_{32}$	$4^{29}/_{32}$ - $4^{25}/_{32}$	5 - $4^7/_8$	$5^1/_8$ - 5	$5^{13}/_{32}$ - $5^5/_{16}$
Yen	$^1/_8$ - $^1/_{32}$	$^1/_8$ - $^1/_{32}$	$^1/_{16}$ - $^1/_{32}$	$^1/_{16}$ - $^1/_{32}$	$^1/_8$ - $^1/_{32}$	$^1/_8$ - $^1/_{32}$
Asian $S	$^1/_4$ - $^1/_8$	$2^1/_4$ - $1^1/_4$	$1^7/_8$ - $1^3/_8$	$2^3/_{32}$ - $1^{19}/_{32}$	$1^{15}/_{16}$ - $1^{11}/_{16}$	$2^3/_8$ - $2^1/_8$

Premiums and Discounts

Another method of quoting forward rates is to specify the amount by which the forward rate differs from the spot rate. The forward rate is said to be at a premium or a discount to the spot rates. *Unfortunately, terminology differs in some countries, notably the UK, and can lead to some confusion.*

UK Terminology

If the quoted currency, i.e. the variable currency, is at a premium in the forward market, this means that it is worth more. Therefore, the base currency is worth a smaller number of units of the quoted currency, and the forward rate is lower than the spot rate. For example, suppose that the sterling/dollar rate is $1.50000 spot and $1.4950 three months forward, the dollar is worth more spot than forward against sterling. In UK terminology, the dollar would be quoted forward three months at a premium of 50 points (0.0050) to the spot rate.

If the quoted currency, i.e. the variable currency, is at a discount in the forward market, it is worth less. Therefore, the base currency is worth a greater number of units of the quoted currency, so the forward rate is higher than the spot rate. For example, suppose that the sterling/drachma spot rate is £1 = Dr490.00 and that the one month forward rate is £1 = Dr493.00, the drachma is worth less spot than one month forward against sterling. In UK terminology, the one-month forward rate is at a discount of three drachmas to the spot rate.

Using the UK meaning of premium and discount

- a premium is subtracted from the spot rate to find the forward rate, and
- a discount is added to the spot rate to find the forward rate.

Alternative Terminology

In other countries, the terms premium and discount have the opposite meaning because they refer to the base currency not the variable currency. To find the forward rate, a premium is added to the spot rate whereas a discount is subtracted.

Why Quote Premiums and Discounts?

It might seem strange that forward rates should be quoted at a premium or a discount to the spot rate, when the actual forward rates could be quoted instead. Premiums and discounts are the preferred method for quoting prices, however, because

- forward differentials, i.e. the size of premium or discount, very often remain unchanged when the spot rate changes. Therefore quoting differentials calls for fewer changes to price information on dealers' information screens

- for many forward transactions, particularly swap transactions, that are described later, the forward differential or swap rate, i.e. the size of the premium or discount, is the key item of information, not the spot or forward rates.

Forward Points

To avoid confusion with the definitions of premium and discount, it is simpler to use the term forward points, or forward adjustment. This is the amount by which the forward rate differs from the spot rate. The quote shows whether the points should be added or subtracted.

Forward points are quoted as a pair of numbers. This represents the dealer's spread, in exactly the same way as for the spot price. The customer always deals on the price that is less favorable to him. When the forward points are applied to the spot price to calculate an outright forward price, this always is done so that the forward price has a wider spread than the spot price to account for the additional risk to the market maker.

- If the forward points are to be deducted from the spot rate, the bank will quote a larger number on the left for the bid rate, and a lower number on the right for the offered rate.
- If the forward points are to be added to the spot rate, the bank will quote a lower number on the left for the bid rate, and a higher number on the right for the offered rate.

Example

The table over the page shows the current FX rates displayed on the rate board in the dealing room of Omega Bank in London.

	£/$	€/$	$/SFr	$/HK$	$/S$
Spot	1.5975-1.5985	1.0610-1.0618	1.4455-1.4465	7.7597-7.7607	1.7755-1.7785
1 month	28-24	36-42	14-10	30-36	81-69
3 months	82-74	108-116	31-25	86-100	235-210
12 months	217-189	245-273	48-40	185-209	582-468

Analysis

The rate board shows, for five exchange rates, the forward points for the one, three and 12 months forward rates against the spot rate.

In the case of the sterling/dollar rate, the forward points are higher on the left than on the right, e.g. 28-24 for the one month forward rate. This means that

- the dollar (variable currency) is worth more forward than spot against sterling (base currency)
- the forward points therefore must be deducted from the spot rate.

£/$ rate

	1 month forward		3 months forward		12 months forward	
Spot rate	1.5975	- 1.5985	1.5975	- 1.5985	1.5975	- 1.5985
Deduct forward points	28	- 24	82	- 74	217	- 189
Forward rate	1.5947	- 1.5961	1.5893	- 1.5911	1.5758	- 1.5796

In the case of the euro/$ exchange rate, the forward points are lower on the left than on the right. For example, the three months forward points for the dollar against the euro are 108-116. This means that

- the dollar (variable currency) is worth less forward than spot against the euro (base currency)
- the forward points therefore must be added to the spot rate to obtain the forward rate.

€/$ rate

	1 month forward		3 months forward		12 months forward	
Spot rate	1.0610	- 1.0618	1.0610	- 1.0618	1.0610	- 1.0618
Add forward points	36	- 42	108	- 116	245	- 273
Forward rate	1.0646	- 1.0660	1.0718	- 1.0734	1.0855	- 1.0891

There is an alternative possibility, not often used, of currency borrowing. This third choice would be to

- obtain a loan in the currency, to mature when the currency receipt is due and convert the loan into domestic currency at today's spot rate
- use the eventual currency receipt to repay the loan and loan interest.

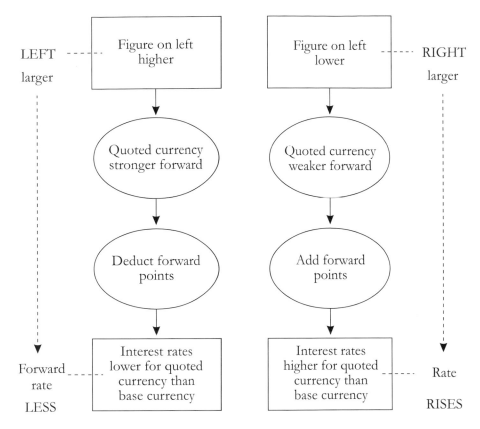

Forward Points and Interest Rates

If the interest rate in country X is *higher* than the interest rate in country y

- the forward rate for quoting the currency of X against the base currency of y will be higher than the spot rate
- the forward rate for quoting the currency of y against the base currency of X will be lower than the spot rate.

In general, weak currencies have higher interest rates and therefore will be quoted forward at a lower value than the spot rate against stronger currencies with a lower interest rate.

It is usual for forward rates to be either at a premium or a discount for all forward contract periods, with the size of premium or discount increasing with the time period to maturity. However, because of differences in the yield curve between two currencies, this sometimes is not the case, the yield curve refers to the interest rates on a currency for different time periods to maturity. For example, suppose that interest rates on one-month borrowing are lower in Japan than in the US, but that three-month interest rates are lower in the US than in Japan. In this situation the yen would be quoted

- at a premium to dollars one-month forward, i.e. lower than the spot rate
- at a discount to dollars three months forward, i.e. higher than the spot rate.

(Note: premium and discount are used here in their UK definitions.)

Premium or Discount Size: Formula

The size of a premium or discount, i.e. the size of the forward points, depends on

- the interest rate differential between the two currencies that can be obtained by reference to eurocurrency interest rates, and
- the time period.

A formula for estimating the size of a premium or discount for forward exchange rates against sterling is as follows

$$\frac{S \times \left[\dfrac{I_Q - I_B}{100}\right] \times \dfrac{D}{365}}{1 + \left[\dfrac{I_B}{100} \times \dfrac{D}{365}\right]}$$

If the quoted currency interest rate is calculated on a 360-day year basis, then this rate must be multiplied by 365/360, to make it compatible with the sterling rate, before substituting in the above equation.

Where

S is the spot rate

D is the number of days forward

I_Q is the interest rate for the quoted currency

I_B is the interest rate of the base currency, in this case, sterling.

- A positive value means the forward points should be added to the spot rate.
- A negative value means the forward points should be subtracted from the spot rate.

A similar formula can be used to estimate premiums or discounts for currencies against the dollar, I_B representing the interest rate on the dollar, and a 360-day year applying instead of 365 days.

To calculate the premium or discount, middle rates are used for the spot rate and the eurocurrency interest rates, to derive a middle price for the forward points. The bid-offer spread then can be made as narrow or wide as necessary, around the middle price for the forward points.

Example
Using the figures below, we can estimate the one-month forward premium for the dollar against sterling for the middle price. We must use the actual number of days that in this case we will assume to be 28 (February).

The following rates are current

Spot £/$: middle rate	1.5937
One month euro-sterling rate	$5^{13}/_{32}$ - $5^{11}/_{32}$
Middle rate	$5^3/_8$ = 5.375
One month eurodollar rate (eurolibor)	$4^1/_{16}$ - $3^{15}/_{16}$
Middle rate	4

Eurodollar interest is calculated on a 360-day year basis, and sterling on a 365-day year basis. For comparative purposes, we must multiply the dollar interest rate by a factor of 365/360.

$$4 \times 365/360 = 4.0556$$

The forward adjustment (forward points), applying the formula, is

$$\frac{1.5937 \times \left[\dfrac{4.0556 - 5.375}{100} \right] \times \dfrac{28}{365}}{1 + \left[\dfrac{5.375}{100} \times \dfrac{28}{365} \right]}$$

$$\frac{1.5937 \times (-0.013194) \times 0.0767}{1.004123} = -0.0016 \text{ or } -16 \text{ points}$$

The value is negative so the forward points should be deducted from the spot rate.

Spot middle rate	1.5937
Deduct forward points	-0.0016
One month forward middle rate	1.5921

Why Use Forward Contracts?

Forward contracts lock in an exchange rate now for a future purchase or sale of currency. It should be remembered that once made, the contract is binding and must be honored, whatever happens to the spot rate in the period up to the settlement (value) date. The following examples illustrate how and why companies use them.

Example 1
A UK company has to pay a supplier €1,000,000 in one month. The spot rate (€/£) is 0.6620-0.6630 and the one-month forward points are 16-24.

1. What rate would the bank quote for a forward contract?
2. What will the company pay for the euros?
3. What can the company do if the spot rate in one month has changed to €1 = £0.6640?

Analysis
1. The bank is selling euros to the company at the more favorable rate to itself, the higher of the two rates, i.e. fewer euros to the pound sterling that is the same as more pounds to one euro, for both spot and forward adjustment. The forward points are larger on the right hand side (offered rate) and therefore are added to the spot rate.

Spot rate	0.6630
Forward points (add)	+ 0.0024
	0.6654

2. The customer must pay (€1,000,000 x 0.6654) = £665,400

3. The customer cannot exploit the more favorable spot rate one month later because the forward contract is binding. If the customer had opted not to take out a forward contract, and had chosen instead to buy the euros one month later at the spot rate of 0.6640 there would have been a currency transaction exposure of €1 million for one month. In this case, the customer would have profited from the exposure and would have paid only £664,000 (£1,400 less) at the eventual spot rate. Forward contracts are for risk-averse companies that recognize the dangers of exchange rates moving adversely and thus creating unacceptable losses.

Example 2
A US company has sold capital equipment to a Swiss customer for an agreed payment of SFr1.5 million in three months. The spot rate ($/SFr) is 2.4646-2.4676 and the three-month forward points are 82-58.

1. What rate would a bank quote for a forward exchange contract?
2. How much would the company eventually receive in dollars?

Analysis
The bank is buying Swiss francs from the US company and will charge the more favorable rate to itself, that is the higher rate. The forward points should be subtracted (left-hand value higher).

1. Spot rate	2.4676
Forward points (three months)	- 0.0058
Forward rate	2.4618

2. Proceeds for the company in dollars:
   SFr1,500,000 at $1 = SFr2.4618 = $609,310.26

Exercise
Provide solutions to the following questions.

A company will receive ¥80 million in one month that it wants to exchange for dollars. The spot rate ($/¥) is 120.590-120.750 and the current one month forward points are 520-560.

1. What forward rate ($/¥) would a bank quote?
2. What will be the company's dollar receipts?

Solution

The bank is buying yen and selling dollars, so it will use the rate on the right-hand side because this gives it more yen for each dollar. The forward points are higher on the right-hand side and therefore should be added.

Spot rate	120.750
Forward points (one month)	+0.560
Forward rate	121.310

Dollar receipts for the company will be ¥80 million at 121.31 per dollar = $659,467.48

Forward Cross Rates

Forward cross rates are forward rates between currencies where neither currency is the dollar. As with spot transactions, most large forward transactions between banks involve the sale or purchase of dollars, and large cross-rate deals are comparatively uncommon. To sell Canadian dollars forward in exchange for sterling, a bank normally would make two transactions

- selling Canadian dollars forward in exchange for dollars
- selling dollars forward in exchange for sterling.

The sterling/Canadian dollar forward rate that is obtained from these transactions is the forward cross rate that can be derived from the dollar/Canadian dollar and sterling/dollar forward rates. Forward rates for non-dollar currencies therefore can be calculated using the dollar forward rates for each currency as a go-between.

Example

For a customer buying yen in exchange for Swiss francs, we can use the following table to determine

1. the spot cross rate (SFr/¥)

2. the three-month forward cross rate (SFr/¥)

Rates against the dollar

	Spot	**3 months forward points**
Yen	122.690-122.750	300-270
Swiss franc	1.5028-1.5038	154-146

Analysis
1. Spot cross rate
   Bank sells ¥ for $ 122.690
   Bank buys SFr for $ 1.5038
        SFr1 = ¥81.587
2. Three-month forward cross rate
   Bank sells ¥ for £   (122.690-0.300)
   Bank buys SFr for $ (1.5038-0.0146)
       — 122.390/1.4892
        SFr1 = ¥82.185

Broken Dates

So far we have used an exact number of months for the forward contract period and forward rates normally are quoted for regular dates, one, two, three, six and 12 months forward. However, a forward deal can be arranged for any future date because a customer might want to receive or pay currency on a *specific* future date that is not an exact number of months away. In this situation, the bank will quote a forward rate for this broken date or odd date.

The forward rate for the contract can be calculated in various ways. One method is to use interpolation. This works on the presumption that the size of the forward points changes at an equal daily rate between one month and the next.

Example
Suppose that now is October 18 and spot and forward rates are

£/$

Spot	1.5135-1.5145
One month	99-97
Two months	187-185
Three months	265-262

Spot value date is October 20

A customer wants to buy $400,000 to make an overseas payment on January 6. What rate would the bank offer?

Analysis

The bank is selling dollars and the forward rate points are

Two months	187 points	(to December 20)
Three months	<u>265</u> points	(to January 20)
Difference	78 points	

From December 20 to January 6 is 17 days.

From December 20 to January 20 is 31 days. Because the forward points increase by 78 points in 31 days between December 20 and January 20, the daily rate of change in the premium is 78/31points.

Therefore the forward points to apply to a contract for delivery on January 6 is

$187 + (78 \times 17/31) = 187 + 43 = 230$ or 2.30 cents. The forward points are deducted.

Spot rate	1.5135
Forward points to January 6	<u>-0.0230</u>
Forward rate	1.4905

Value Date Option Contracts (Time Options)

Sometimes a company cannot specify a *precise* date for an anticipated receipt or payment of currency. Value date option contracts give the customer an option on the value date for the forward contract, and are called option forwards or time options by interbank FX dealers. The bank will offer a forward exchange contract but will give the customer the *option* to receive the currency on any working day between two agreed dates. The value date for the contract is decided by the customer but must be within the earliest and latest option dates of the contract.

Example

Date: 18 October

Spot rate £/NZ$	2.5875-2.5925
One-month forward	75-62
Two months forward	137-125
Three months forward	187-175

A company anticipates a requirement for NZ$600,000 some time between December 20 and January 20.

With a value date option contract for the bank to sell NZ$600,000 at any time between these two dates two to three months ahead, a bank will quote either the two-month or the three-month forward rate.

The rate chosen by the bank will be the rate most favorable to itself

- for selling currency – the lower of the two rates
- for buying currency – the higher of the two rates.

The more favorable rate, two months or three months forward, depends on whether the currency is quoted forward at a premium or discount.

In this example

Two-month forward rate   2.5875-0.0137 = 2.5738

Three-month forward rate   2.5875-0.0187 = 2.5688

2.5688 is the lower of the two rates and therefore is the selling price quoted by the bank. The customer will pay £233,572.10 (600,000 ÷ 2.5688) for the New Zealand dollars.

Exercise

Using the same figures from the previous example, what would a bank quote for buying New Zealand dollars from a company at any date between November 20 and January 20?

Solution

One-month forward rate   2.5925 - 0.0125 = 2.5800

Three-month forward rate   2.5925 - 0.0175 = 2.5750

2.5800 is the higher of the two rates and is therefore the buying price quoted by the bank.

A bank is asked to quote prices for a value date option contract for settlement at any time between two future dates, an earlier Date 1 and a later Date 2.

	Bank sells currency	**Bank buys currency**
Currency quoted forward at premium	Forward rate = rate for Date 2	Forward rate = rate for Date 1
Currency quoted forward at discount	Forward rate = rate for Date 1	Forward rate = rate for Date 2

The advantage of a forward value date option to a company is its flexibility. The company can lock in a fixed exchange rate at which it knows it can deal. There is no exposure to interest rate changes that would affect it if its commitments were covered with an ordinary forward exchange contract (a forward outright) for a specific value date, that subsequently needed to be adjusted by means of extending the contract. The disadvantage is the cost, given the wide bid/offer spread that is involved, particularly if the period of the option is wide.

Cost of Forward Cover

A bank aims to generate a profit from buying and selling currency that it does from the spread between its bid and offer prices.

With this proviso, arranging a forward contract does not have an obvious cost to the customer. If it did, companies would be more reluctant to use it, and more inclined to gamble on the currency risk, waiting to buy or sell currency at the spot rate as and when required, instead of arranging a forward contract in advance.

There is the implied cost, however, of being unable to benefit from favorable spot exchange rate movements once a forward contract has been arranged because the forward contract is binding and locks in an exchange rate.

Outright and Swap Operations

Forward exchange transactions are made for one of two main reasons

- to cover a future requirement to buy or sell a currency arising from a commercial or a financial transaction
- in connection with money market operations, borrowing and lending in foreign currencies, that involve a simultaneous spot purchase and forward sale, or simultaneous spot sale and forward purchase.

FX dealers distinguish between these two types of transaction, referring to a single forward transaction as an outright operation and a simultaneous spot purchase and forward sale as a swap operation.

FX Transactions (see diagram on page 84)
Note: Short-dated forward swaps that involve settlement before spot value date, are described later.

Swap Rate
The difference between the spot rate and the forward rate is the forward adjustment or forward points. The forward points reflect the differential between the interest rates in the two currencies. In a forward swap transaction, the forward points are referred to as the *swap*.

- If the forward rate is lower than the spot rate, the counterparty buying the *base* currency spot and selling it forward will make a loss equal to the swap points and is said to pay the points. The counterparty selling the base currency spot and buying it forward makes a profit.

83

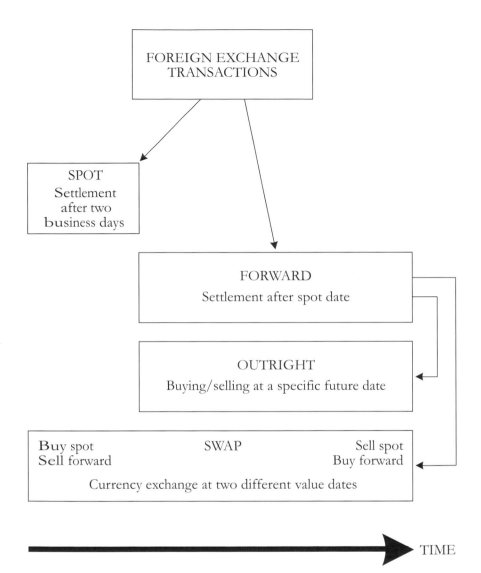

- If the forward rate is higher than the spot rate, the counterparty buying the *base* currency spot and selling it forward makes a profit equal to the swap point, and is said to make the points. The counterparty selling the base currency spot and buying it forward makes a loss.

Example

Omega Bank arranges a forward swap transaction to sell $10 million spot against Hong Kong dollars and buy them three months forward. The spot rate for $/HK$ is $1 = HK$7.7630 and the three-month forward rate is $1 = HK$7.7737.

Analysis
The forward rate is higher than the spot rate by HK$0.0107 or 107 points (7.7737-7.7630). The base currency here is dollars, and the variable currency is Hong Kong dollars. Omega Bank is selling the base currency spot, and will make a loss *in Hong Kong dollars* equal to the swap rate of 107 points.

	HK$
Sell $100 million at 7.7630	776,300,000
Buy $100 million at 7.7737	777,370,000
Loss (in HK$)	1,070,000
(Loss = 100 million x 0.0107)	

Calculating the Forward Swap Points
The cost of making a forward swap depends on the interest rate differential between the two currencies.

A formula for calculating the forward swap points is as follows:

$$\text{Forward (swap) points} = \frac{S \times \left[\dfrac{I_V - I_B}{100} \right] \times \dfrac{D}{360*}}{1 + \left[\dfrac{I_B}{100} \times \dfrac{D}{360*} \right]}$$

* 365 for sterling and Australian dollars

Where
    S is the spot exchange rate
    I_B is the interest rate obtainable in the base currency
    I_V is the interest rate obtainable in the variable currency
    D is the number of days forward

● If the result is a negative value, the interest rate in the base currency is higher than the interest rate in the variable currency. The base currency is deducted from the spot rate to obtain the forward rate.

- If the result is a positive value, the interest rate in the base currency is lower than the interest rate in the variable currency. Therefore the base currency is worth more forward than spot, and the forward points should be added to the spot rate to obtain the forward rate.

An adjustment to interest rates has to be made for calculating the forward points when interest in one currency is quoted on a 360-day basis and interest in the other is calculated on a 365-day basis. Suppose for example that interest on the dollar is 4% and on sterling interest is 6% per annum. If interest is earned for a whole year (365 days), interest per £100 invested would be £6, but interest per $100 invested would be

$$\$100 \text{ x } 4\% \text{ x } 365/360 = \$4.056$$

Therefore an adjustment has to be made to make the interest rates properly comparable.

Interest rate adjustments

Base currency interest	Variable currency interest	Adjustment to variable currency interest
360 days	360 days	None
360 days	365 days	x 360/365
365 days	365 days	None
365 days	360 days	x 365/360

Example 1
The spot sterling/dollar rate is $1.4811. A rate of 4% per annum is obtainable on the dollar and a rate of 6% per annum is obtainable on sterling.

Analysis
The adjusted dollar interest rate is 4.056% (see example opposite). The forward points for three months, i.e. the premium or discount for a three-month forward contract, is as follows, assuming there are 91 days between the spot value and forward value dates.

Sterling is the base currency.

$$\frac{1.4811 \times \left[\dfrac{4.056 - 6}{100}\right] \times \dfrac{91}{365}}{1 + \left[\dfrac{6}{100} \times \dfrac{91}{365}\right]}$$

$$= \frac{-0.007178}{1.0149589} = -0.0071 \text{ (i.e. 71 points)}$$

The value is negative, therefore the points are deducted from the spot rate to obtain the forward rate. The three-month forward rate will be 1.4740 (1.4811 - 0.0071).

Example 2
The currency dollar/Mexican peso spot rate is 9.5500. The six-month interest rate on the dollar is 3.5% per annum and the six-month rate for the peso is 8.5%.

Analysis
The swap points for a six-month forward contract, assuming a period of 184 days, is as follows. The dollar is the base currency.

$$\text{Forward points} = \frac{9.5500 \times \left[\dfrac{8.5 - 3.5}{100}\right] \times \dfrac{184}{365}}{1 + \left[\dfrac{3.5}{100} \times \dfrac{184}{365}\right]}$$

$$= \frac{+0.2441}{1.01789} = +0.2398$$

The value is positive, and the base currency is worth more forward than spot. The forward (swap) points should be added to the spot rate to obtain the forward rate. The forward rate should be 9.7898 (9.5500 + 0.2398).

How a Bank Covers a Forward Deal

When a bank deals with a company for an outright forward date, in other words, when it arranges a forward contract for a specific future date, it usually considers that it has a position in the currency and often will wish to cover its own exposure. It has several ways in which to do this.

- It might cover both the spot and forward deals: the bank's spot dealer will cover the spot side and the forward dealer will cover the forward. For example, if a bank transacts to buy $50 million three months' forward in exchange for sterling, it can arrange to sell $50 million for spot immediately, and would cover the forward exposure by means of a swap, buying $50 million spot and simultaneously selling the same amount forward.

- It might cover the spot deal only: if the spot dealer feels that the spot side of the deal is a risk and will incur a loss by maintaining that position, the position will be covered. The forward dealer, however, might feel that interest rate structures will move in his/her favor and therefore decide to leave the position open. For example, if a bank transacts to buy $50 million three months' forward in exchange for sterling, it might sell $50 million spot.

- It might cover the forward swap only: if the forward dealer expects interest rate structures to move against him/her, the deal will be covered immediately. The spot dealer, on the other hand, might expect the exchange rate to move in his/her favor and therefore will want to maintain the position.

- It might leave the position completely exposed: if both dealers expect the rates to move in favor, the position may be left exposed.

- The bank might take the position into its books: if the spot dealer already has taken a position that is the opposite of the new commitment to the customer, he/she may decide to use that commitment to reduce the current position. For example, if the bank's spot dealer has sold more dollars than have been purchased in exchange for sterling, he/she can use a new order for the customer to sell dollars and buy sterling to reduce the overall dollar exposure.

7

Closeouts and Extensions

Unforeseen circumstances can arise even in the best managed companies. When dealing with foreign currency transactions

- receipts or payments can be delayed
- anticipated receipts or payments could fail to materialize. Customers can go out of business, and fail to pay due debts.

When this happens, any company that has made a forward exchange contract with its bank is contractually bound to execute the existing contract.

Therefore the company must ask its bank to

- closeout the forward contract
- extend the forward contract to roll back the cover to a later date
- arrange two other forward contracts, to pull forward the cover to an earlier date.

If the customer's cash transaction	Course of action
will no longer occur	closeout
will not occur at the expected time and might not occur at all	closeout
will occur later than expected	extend forward contract
will occur earlier than expected	pull forward the cover

Banking practise varies, but most banks follow these outlines for closeout or extension of forward exchange contracts.

Closeout of a Forward Contract

Closeout is the action a bank takes to complete a forward exchange contract when the other party (the customer) is unable or unwilling to meet its obligations under the contract. A closeout can be transacted only with the counterparty bank to the original transaction.

The bank arranges for the customer to perform its part of the forward exchange contract by selling or buying the missing currency at the forward rate for the maturity date of the contract.

The customer's bank account will register a single entry for the difference between the two transactions. This could be a debit or a credit, because the difference between the forward contract rate and the spot rate could give the customer a loss or a gain on the closeout.

Closeout will be required in one of the following situations when the customer

- is unable to obtain any of the foreign currency it has arranged to sell to the bank, or no longer requires any of the foreign currency it has contracted for purchase from the bank, or
- cannot obtain *all* of the foreign currency contracted for sale to the bank, or no longer requires *all* of the foreign currency contracted for purchase from the bank.

Example
On March 5, a UK company expects to receive $350,000 in three months. It makes a forward exchange contract agreement with its bank to sell the dollars for sterling, at a rate of 1.4685, derived as follows

Spot rate on March 5	1.4955
3 months forward points (forward points deducted)	- 0.0270
Outright price for June 7 settlement	1.4685

On April 17, the company learns the money will not be received because its customer is refusing to pay.

On request, the bank will *closeout* the forward exchange contract on the maturity date in such a way as to protect itself.

- It will keep the company to its forward contract, and on June 7 will buy $350,000 from the company at £1 = $1.4685.
- It will sell the company a matching $350,000 at the forward rate for June 7. The net cost or gain to the company will be debited or credited to its account at the bank.

If, on April 17, the forward rate for June 7 is 1.4610-1.4620 the closeout arrangement will be as follows

	£
Bank buys $350,000 at £1 = $1.4685	238,338.44
Bank closes out contract by selling $350,000 at 1.4610	239,561.94
Net cost to customer (in £)	1,223.50

If, on April 17, the forward rate on June 7 is 1.4800-1.4810 the closeout arrangement will be

	£
Bank buys $350,000 at £1 = $1.4685	238,338.44
Bank closes out contract by selling $350,000 at 1.4800	236,486.49
Net gain to customer (in £)	1,851.95

Extending a Forward Exchange Contract

A company might find that on the value date of a forward exchange contract, it will not receive or will not yet have to pay the expected currency, and wishes to defer its delivery date. In this situation, the bank might offer to extend (roll forward) the contract.

An extension of a forward exchange contract is a forward swap transaction. The customer:

- sells currency spot and simultaneously buys the same quantity forward, or

● buys the currency spot and simultaneously sells it forward.

A forward swap also can involve selling or buying currency forward and buying or selling the same amount forward for a later settlement date, i.e. a forward swap can involve two forward transactions rather than one spot and one forward transaction. An extension involving a spot purchase or sale means that the customer has delayed extending the forward contract until the last possible moment.

The first part of the forward will closeout the old contract. What makes an extension different from a closeout is that the bank will arrange a new forward exchange contract with the customer for the extension period *at a rate that is more favorable to the customer* than for an ordinary forward exchange contract.

This is because the customer is doing a forward swap. The bank has an interest rate risk from the transaction, but no spot market risk, and so does not need to charge the spot bid/offer spread.

● If the bank is selling currency, it will quote its spot buying rate (offer rate) plus or minus its forward selling premium or discount.
● If the bank is buying currency, it will apply the current buying premium or discount to its spot selling rate (bid rate).

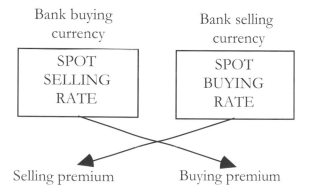

In practise, the middle rate often is used for spot part of the swap.

This is known as the diagonal rule, and the forward rate of exchange applied to an extension of a forward contract is as follows.

Example
A UK company sold goods to a buyer in the US for $500,000. Payment was expected on November 3, and the company took out a three-month forward contract on August 1 to sell the currency to its bank. However, payment did not arrive on time, and on November 1 the company asked its bank to extend the contract by one month, for settlement on December 3.

The payment eventually was received and the contract was settled on December 3.

Currency Rates (£/$)

	Spot	**one-month forward**	**three-month forward**
1 August	$1.4850-1.4860	-	2.26-2.23
1 November	$1.4460-1.4470	0.94-0.92	

Analysis
The original three-month forward contract on August 1 was for $500,000, delivery on November 3, at a forward rate of 1.4637.

Spot rate	1.4860
3-month forward points (deduct)	- 0.0223
Forward rate	1.4637

This would be expected to produce a sterling return of £341,600.05.

On November 1, the company asks its bank to extend the contract, this it does by closing out the old contract and arranging a new contract at a favorable rate.

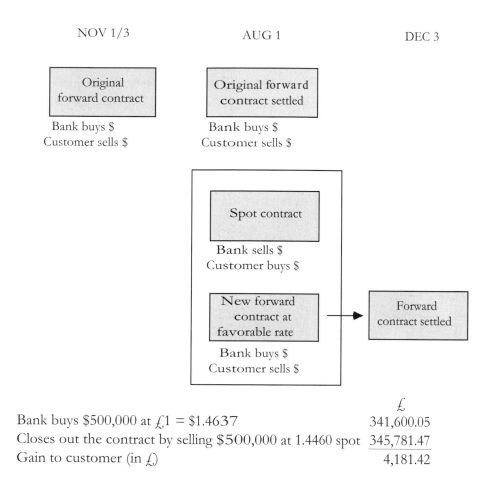

NOV 1/3	AUG 1	DEC 3
Original forward contract	Original forward contract settled	
Bank buys $	Bank buys $	
Customer sells $	Customer sells $	

Spot contract

Bank sells $
Customer buys $

New forward contract at favorable rate

Bank buys $
Customer sells $

Forward contract settled

	£
Bank buys $500,000 at £1 = $1.4637	341,600.05
Closes out the contract by selling $500,000 at 1.4460 spot	345,781.47
Gain to customer (in £)	4,181.42

The bank extends the contract by one month to December 3. It is buying dollars, and so the rate is as follows

Selling rate spot (on November 1)	1.4460
1-month forward points, buying rate (deduct)	-0.0092
Forward rate for extension	1.4368

On December 3, the bank will buy the $500,000 (at £1 = $1.4368) for £347,995.55.

Pulling Forward Cover
A company could find that the date for an anticipated foreign currency receipt or payment is changed to an earlier time. In such a situation,

cover can be brought forward by means of

- an equal and *opposite* shorter-term forward contract expiring on the same date as the original contract, with either the original or a different counterparty bank, and
- a forward contract for the expected income or payment, for settlement on the revised date.

Pulling forward cover, like a forward contract extension, is a forward swap transaction.

Example

A company contracts on June 1 Year 1 to sell forward $5 million into sterling for value June 3 Year 2, as a hedge against the contracted forward sale of its products to a US customer. However, in September, the customer wishes to change the settlement date to December 3 Year 1, because the US customer has agreed to pay in advance.

Analysis

To pull the cover forward from June 3 Year 2 to December 3 Year 1, a further two forward contracts would be transacted. Details are as follows.

	Spot rate (£/$)	Forward value date	Forward premium
June 1 Year 1	1.4995-1.5005	June 3 Year 2 (sell dollars)	425-417
September 1 Year 1	1.4615-1.4625	June 3 Year 2 (buy dollars)	375-370
		December 3 Year 1 (sell dollars)	150-142

1. *Original contract (transaction date June 1 Year 1)*
   The company sells forward $5 million to a bank, Omega Bank, at 1.4588 (1.5005-0.0417) for value June 3 Year 4. Expected sterling return = £3,427,476.64

2. *Adjustment contracts (transaction date September 1 Year 1)*
   The company now transacts an equal and opposite contract for
   the same value date as the original contract that is June 3 Year 2.
   Therefore it buys forward $5 million from another bank, Zeta
   Bank, at 1.4250 (1.4625*-0.0375) for value on June 3 Year 2.
   Sterling cost = £3,508,771.93.

   Simultaneously, the company transacts a new forward contract
   to sell forward the $5 million to Zeta Bank for value on the
   required forward date that is now December 3 Year 1. The
   forward rate is 1.4483 (1.4625-0.0142), and the expected sterling
   return = £3,452,323.41.

   *Note. The transaction with Zeta Bank, involving a forward sale
   and a forward purchase of dollars, is a form of forward swap
   transaction. Because the company is arranging a forward swap,
   the diagonal rule applies and it will obtain a more favorable rate.
   In this example, the bank's buying rate, rather than the bank's
   spot selling rate 1.4615, is applied.

   In practise, the middle rate, in this example 1.4620, is often
   used for both parts of the swap, and the appropriate number of
   forward points applied. The end result is that the company is
   paying 233 swap points for the transaction, as follows

Part 1 of swap, value June 3 Year 2:	
Forward points to buy dollars	-375
Part 2 of swap, value December 3 Year 1:	
Forward points to sell dollars	-142
Swap points (difference, = -375 - (-142)	-233

3. *Net effect*

	£
£ return, June 3 Year 2 - Omega Bank	3,427,474.64
£ cost, June 3 Year 2 - Zeta Bank	(3,508,771.93)
£ return, December 3 Year 1 - Zeta Bank	3,452,323.41
Net income (in £)	3,371,026.12

Instead of pulling forward cover by making adjusting forward contracts with a second bank, it would be easier to amend the original forward contract with the original counterparty bank. This bank could agree to a buy-back and amendment of the original contract. However, a bank that is asked to do this will know that it has placed its customer in a vulnerable position and may quote an uncompetitive rate. For this reason, large companies that transact regularly with several banks often prefer the more complex process of using a second bank to pull forward cover.

Alternatives to Pulling Forward Cover

There are two alternatives to use in these situations.

Alternative 1. The company takes delivery of the dollars at the rearranged earlier delivery date, December 3 Year 1, and puts enough on deposit in a dollar account, earning interest until June 3 Year 2, to meet the company's obligations under the forward exchange contract. The interest earned will create extra dollar income, and the surplus dollars can be sold.

This method is suitable only if the company is willing to hold this quantity of cash, about $5 million, on deposit between December 3 Year 1 and June 3 Year 2, denying its deployment as part of the working capital of the company.

Alternative 2. The company takes delivery of the dollars and sells them at the spot rate. Suppose that this is £1 = $1.4700. At the same time, it would execute a forward exchange contract to purchase the same amount ($5 million) to the original end date (June 3 Year 2). The forward rate might be 1.4450. This alternative, however, leaves the company exposed to changes in interest rates during the period, until the adjustment contracts are transacted upon receipt of the dollars.

The two forward contracts will net out in foreign currency terms, leaving the company with the proceeds of its spot sale, plus or minus the difference between the proceeds and the payment for the forward contracts on June 3.

	£	£
December 3 Year 1		
Sale of $5 million spot (at 1.4700)		3,401,361
June 3 Year 2		
Purchase of $5 million at 1.4450	3,460,208	
Sale of $5 million at 1.4588	3,427,475	
Net cost		- 32,733
Total proceeds (in £)		3,368,628

Problems Matching Forward Contracts to Cash Flow
Several problems arise when trying to match forward contracts to cash flow, by pulling the forward cover to an earlier date.

- There are *logistical problems* of monitoring the situation, making the necessary transactions to maintain a portfolio of forward cover, and knowing which forward contracts apply to which situations. These pose particular problems for companies wanting to use forward contracts regularly and in significant quantity. Remember that with pulling forward cover, there are three forward contracts for one underlying trade transaction.
- *Credit commitment.* Bank credit lines will be tied up for the transacted amounts. In the case of pulling the forward cover to an earlier date, the credit lines tied up will represent a value of three times the amount of the original transaction.
- *Cash flow.* The actual cash flow will not equal the amount originally anticipated because of movements in the exchange rate between the transaction dates.

8

Swap Transactions and Short-dated Forward Transactions

Swap transactions developed from outright forward exchange contracts.

A swap transaction is an agreement to exchange a fixed amount of one currency for another, at an agreed rate of exchange, and a *simultaneous* agreement to re-exchange the same fixed amount of the first currency at a later date for the other currency, also at an agreed rate of exchange. Therefore it consists of two transactions, simultaneously executed; for example, a spot sale and forward purchase, or a spot purchase and forward sale.

Elements of an FX Swap

In an FX swap transaction

- there are two exchanges of currency
- there is a different value date for each exchange of currency
- the first transaction occurs on the near date
- the reverse transaction occurs on the far date
- there is a different exchange rate for each exchange of currency.

The first transaction, at the near date, is often a spot transaction. A swap transaction can be arranged between a bank and its customer, or between banks. An extension of a forward contract is an example of an FX swap transaction.

Swap Price
In a swap transaction, because the same fixed amount of base currency

will be re-exchanged, it is the *difference* between the two exchange rates that matters more than the exchange rates themselves. This difference in the two rates is called the *swap price*.

This type of swap transaction must not be confused with currency swaps that are the subject of another title in this series.

Example
A company arranges a swap transaction with a bank to buy $5,000,000 now. Simultaneously, it agrees to sell back the dollars in six months' time.

The exchange rate is

	Spot rate	six-month forward
£/$ rate	1.5730-40	3.61-3.56

The agreed exchange rate for the near-date exchange is the bank's spot selling rate for dollars. Alternatively, another rate might be agreed, such as the mid-price between the spot selling and buying rates. Assume that the agreed rate for the first part of the swap transaction is 1.5735.

In this example, the purchase and sale of the dollars will give a profit to the customer, because the price at which the dollars are sold is better than the price paid. The difference will be the smaller of the two prices in the swap quote, i.e. 3.56 rather than 3.61. The rate for the far-date transaction is 1.5735-0.0356 = 1.5379.

Spot transaction, near date:

  Company buys $5m for (5m ÷ 1.5735)   £3,177,629.49

Forward transaction, far date:

  Company sells $5m for (5m ÷ 1.5379)   £3,251,186.68

It might seem that in this example the bank has lost out on the transaction because it will buy the dollars for a higher amount than it sold them. However, its profit comes from being able to invest or lend the sterling for six months at a higher rate of interest than it could have earned on the dollar, with the swap transaction protecting it from any currency exposure.

Why are Swap Transactions Used?

Swap transactions can benefit both companies and banks in interbank deals.

- A company or a bank might have a surplus or shortage of a currency for a foreseeable period. For example, a UK company might have excess dollars for two months. Because it needs the dollars in two months' time, it can arrange a swap, selling the dollars now in exchange for sterling and buying them back at an agreed rate after two months. The sterling can be invested for two months and the company will have managed its short-term exposure in dollars.
- Swap transactions sometimes can be used to profit from favorable interest rate differentials that might exist to switch surplus funds, or investment funds, short term into a currency that offers a more attractive rate of interest. This is possible only if the company can obtain better interest rates, relative to interbank rates, in one currency rather than another.

Swap transactions are used by banks to hedge against currency exposures in interbank deals, when they are long in one currency and short in another, for a foreseeable time period.

- A long position means the bank has more of the currency than it needs.
- A short position means the bank will have to buy the currency to meet foreseeable obligations.

If a bank's dealer deliberately runs a long position in a currency, he or she is speculating that the currency will appreciate in value. A deliberate short position is speculating that the currency will depreciate. To avoid having to speculate, a bank can arrange a swap transaction with another bank selling the currency in which it is currently long in exchange for the currency in which it is currently short, with an agreement to reverse the transaction at a future date.

Short Dates

Forward value dates earlier than one month are referred to as short dates. Some short dates are even earlier than the spot value date (two working days ahead). Even though settlement is required *before* spot value date, these transactions, oddly enough, are nevertheless called short-dated forwards. Short-dated FX transactions are commonly used by banks and large companies as part of their daily management of very short-term currency cash flows. Each day banks must be certain that they have all the currency they need to meet their payment and lending obligations; if there is a short-term surplus of currency, this can be sold or lent. Both the eurocurrency markets, lending and borrowing, and the FX markets, buying and selling, are used for this currency-management process.

- Interbank FX deals for short dates, like short-term eurocurrency borrowing and lending arrangements, help banks to arrange their foreign currency position each day.
- When a spot transaction is arranged, value date for the exchange of currencies should be two days later. Banks or large companies, however, often will want currencies to be exchanged more quickly, with value today or value tomorrow, not in two days.

Example
Company Z anticipates having to make a payment of $20 million on March 11 and buys this amount of currency spot on March 9 for value March 11, two working days later. Several hours later it becomes apparent that payment is actually required on March 10. Company Z has two alternatives.

- It can borrow $20 million from March 10 to 11 at the prevailing eurodollar interest rate. If this loan were arranged on the afternoon of March 9 it would be known as a *Tom-next* borrowing because the loan is from tomorrow until the next day.

- It can effect a foreign currency buy-and-sell transaction by agreeing to buy $20 million for value March 10 and selling $20 million for value March 11. This gives Company Z the required amount a day earlier than previously arranged. The cost of this adjustment would be one day's interest, in the form of a points premium or discount. If such a transaction is made on the afternoon of March 9 it would be known as a Tom-next FX swap because there is a purchase for value tomorrow and a sale for value the next day.

The counterparties to the transaction exchange currencies, but receive value on different dates. If might be helpful therefore to think of a short-dated transaction as an agreement to buy and sell currency, but with an element of short-term lending involved because one counterparty will be receiving value before having to give value back.

Of the two alternatives, the currency deposit or borrowing is more straightforward because it involves less administration and flow of funds, making these short-dated transactions much more common than short-dated FX swap transactions. However, a swap may be cheaper because only one market maker's spread is paid instead of two, in the case of a loan and deposit.

There are certain regular short dates that are quoted commonly in interbank dealing, using terminology taken from eurocurrency market dealings.

In the eurocurrency market

Overnight means a loan or deposit from today until tomorrow
Tom-next means a loan or deposit from tomorrow until the next day
(spot)
Spot-next means a loan or deposit from spot until the next day.

Tomorrow means the next working day after today, and next means the next working day following.

The same terminology is used in the foreign exchange markets because the premium or discount rates are calculated on the basis of the deposit/loan rate differentials between the two currencies. Thus the term Tom-next is applied both to FX swap transactions and to currency deposits or borrowings.

Short-dated forward transactions can be either

- outright transactions, involving the purchase or sale of currency for a near value date other than spot value date, or
- forward swaps, involving a simultaneous purchase and sale of the same amount of currency, with settlement of both the purchase and the sale side of the transaction on different near value dates, one of which can be the spot value date.

Short-dated forward swap transactions are commonly one of the following

- *Overnight (O/N)*. Overnight transactions have two value dates, one today and one tomorrow. A bank might buy one currency for value today and sell it back for value tomorrow. Alternatively, a bank might sell one currency for value today and contract to buy it back for value tomorrow. Overnight transactions could be described as today/tomorrow.
- *Tom-next (T/N)*. This is a transaction for value dates, tomorrow and the next day. Tom-next is a generic term used for almost any transaction arranged on Day 1 for the sale or deposit or loan of a currency on Day 2, with a reversing transaction on Day 3. When two banks make a Tom-next transaction, they agree to exchange currencies, with one bank buying currency X against currency Y tomorrow and selling currency X against currency Y the day after.
- *Spot-next (S/N)*. Here, the two value dates are the spot value date (two working days ahead) and the day following.

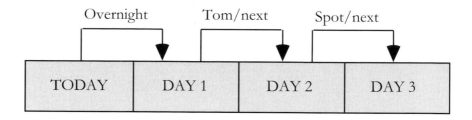

FX dealers also use the terms value today, value tomorrow, and value spot-next, to indicate the value date for a short-dated outright forward transaction.

Deals can be done for value tomorrow in most currencies, but cannot always be done for value today. For example, when the London and European markets open, Japanese banks have already closed their books for today, so deals in yen can be done only for value tomorrow at the earliest. Even the market in London for value tomorrow generally closes during the morning. However, deals for value today can be done in London for sterling/dollars because the UK is ahead of the US in time, and UK banks do not close their books until around 3pm local time.

Value Spot Next

Suppose that sterling interest rates are higher than dollar rates so that the dollar is at a premium to sterling, sterling will be worth fewer dollars in the future than now.

£/$

Spot rate	1.6103-13
Overnight	½ - ¼
Tom-next	½ - ¼
Spot-next	½ - ¼

For an outright short-dated forward transaction for value the next day after spot value day – in three days' time – there will be a premium of ½ - ¼. The customer would be offered the following rates

	Purchase of $ Sale of £	Sale of $ Purchase of £
Spot rate	1.610300	1.611300
Deduct spot-next forward points	-0.000050	-0.000025
Forward rate	1.610250	1.611275

Value Tomorrow

For an outright forward transaction for value tomorrow, one day *before* spot value date, the tom-next forward points are applied. These points should be added in this case, not subtracted. The rate of discount or premium is also reversed, with the offer rate premium/discount applied to the spot bid rate, and the bid rate premium/discount applied to the spot offer rate. The reason for these reversals is because value date occurs *before* the spot value date, not after spot value date. Using the rates in the table above, the customer would be offered the following rates for an outright forward transaction for value tomorrow:

	Purchase of $ Sale of £	Sale of $ Purchase of £
Spot rate	1.610300	1.61130
Add one-day tom-next points	+0.000025	+0.00005
Rate for value tomorrow	1.610325	1.61135

Value Today

For an outright forward transaction with value today, two days before spot value date, the same principle applies, except that the forward points should be for two days, the overnight and the tom-next points. Using the same rates as in the previous examples, the rate quoted to a customer for value trading today will be

	Purchase of $ Sale of £	Sale of $ Purchase of £
Spot rate	1.61030	1.61130
Add forward points for two days (overnight and tom-next)	+0.00005	+0.00010
Rate for value today	1.61035	1.61140

9

Making a Forward Transaction

Arranging a forward exchange contract is done in much the same way as a spot currency transaction.

A small company will contact its local bank that will phone the bank's local area FX dealing center. A forward rate will be agreed by phone. The transaction then must be confirmed in writing, the local bank talking to the customer and the FX center simultaneously.

The bank's local dealing center will access the latest forward rates on its dealing screens that probably will give the bank's month-by-month forward rates over the next 12-month period for each currency against the dollar and sterling. This data will be supplied by the bank's main dealing center and continually updated. This in-house screen also is likely to show value dates for each month, taking account of weekends and bank holidays, so that the customer can be told the exact date on which the exchange of currencies will take place.

Companies with regular but small FX transactions will have a direct dealing link with their bank's local FX dealing center. Large companies dealing regularly in large amounts will have direct access to major FX dealers in banks, and will use on-line data screens for the latest prices.

Quoting a Price

Forward rates, as we have seen, are constructed from the spot rate by subtracting a premium or adding a discount. They are volatile, changing continually, chiefly because of movements in spot rates. Interest rate differentials are more stable and although premiums and discounts change, they do so with less speed and regularity.

Smaller companies that arrange forward contracts with their bank are likely to be given the all-in forward price, without a division into spot rate and premium or discount. When the bank quotes a forward price on the phone, the company must accept it or say no immediately. The company's finance director or financial controller should have reached a decision *before* calling the bank about an acceptable price, and should be prepared to act quickly if an acceptable price is offered.

Example
The financial controller of a company, wishing to sell about €5 million in exchange for dollars, phoned the regional FX dealing center of the company's bank on May 23 and was quoted a forward rate of €1 = $1.0585 for a value date option contract for settlement between July 12 and July 31. The financial controller wished to check whether this rate would be acceptable to the company's finance director and, shortly after leaving the office, was informed by the bank that the rate had already changed to 1.0575. In this case, the company's short delay in agreeing the deal reduced its income by about $5,000 because of the adverse movement of the rate. In other circumstances, the rate might have moved favorably.

Larger companies and banks should be much more concerned about the *size of premium or discount* in forward rates, because a bank might be willing to offer competitive premiums or discounts, and there is potential for large cost savings or higher revenue.

FX screens in the dealing rooms of banks and large companies will indicate the latest forward premiums and discounts, and a corporate dealer normally will seek initially to obtain a quote from several banks on the premium or discount for a forward transaction, rather than ask for an all-in price.

Some screen pages are used more frequently than others because they contain information on competitive current market prices. One such screen page for forward rates is the Barclays screen on Reuters – an example is reproduced opposite.

Large corporate dealers use screens as a guide to check prices offered by banks. Although they are current, a different price could be quoted when a dealer calls a bank to arrange a large forward transaction. The dealer can check any difference, and query the reason if it is large, but cannot insist on obtaining the price shown on the screen.

Small companies without dealing screens should consult the daily financial press before arranging a deal, in order to check the price the bank is quoting. If the bank's quote differs substantially from published rates, the company should ask for an explanation.

Credit Limits

No matter how large or small a customer, a bank will consider itself at risk with its FX contracts because customers can default on agreements. Therefore a bank will fix limits on the amount it is willing to deal, both spot and forward, with a customer.

- A bank's risk on any deal will depend on the face value of the deal, the period to maturity and the volatility of the two currencies.
- The bank may ask its credit controller to assess a customer's creditworthiness for a particularly large or unusual transaction.

Rates are indicative only, and FX dealers are not obliged to trade at the rates shown for their bank on the information screens.

Reuters FX Information Screen

Time of day (in GMT) of the quotes shown on screen. Real time quotes.

The spot £/$ rate quoted by Barclays Bank at this time on 9 June. A large customer could sell large blocks of dollars at 1.6016 and buy dollars at 1.6006

Reuters' page code

	SPOT	1 MTH	2 MTHS	3 MTHS	6 MTHS	12 MTHS
USD	1.6006/16	4.75/2.75	6.25/3.25	6/3	5/10	32.5/42.5
EUR	0.6517/26	13/16	27/30	42/46	81/87	163/175
CHF	2.4389/22	93/84	178/167	269/255	507/486	974/944
JPY	190.31/60	87/82	168/161	256/247	494/480	992/965
SEK	13.675/10	28/22	54/44	81/69	152/131	283/250
NOK	12.587/03	13/26	21/36	33/50	49/74	43/81
DKK	11.385/01	26/14	48/35	71/56	129/109	248/208
AUD	2.4196/49	13/2	21/4	27/10	31/1	-43/+29
NZD	3.0018/94	26/5	47/13	60/26	94/27	136/4
CAD	2.3599/31	13/6	23/13	31/18	44/3	-45/+3
ZAR	9.742/845	723/784	1361/1542	188/223	371/407	725/781
SAR	6.0018.77	-7/+14	12/36	45/70	174/215	542/628
HKD	12.4142/37	-34/+22	-21/+83	33/177	431/631	1583/2145
SGD	2.7389/55	167/3	235/69	307/141	522/272	847/509
THB	58.92/29	-13/+18	-24/+35	-40/+58	-28/+87	-51/+194
IDR	12212/701	88/235	159/418	275/599	356/1162	746/2042
GRD	496.23/03	125/252	288/435	457/638	760/1177	758/1754

13.52 BARCLAYS BANK PLC LONDON   UK36022   BARCBAST
STERLING RATES   INDEX <BARCFX>

<BARCBASV>

The left-hand column shows the exchange rate being quoted. $ is the sterling/dollar rate.

Other lines show the rates against sterling for the euro, Swiss franc, yen, Swedish krona, Norwegian krone and so on.

Forward points are the premiums or discounts for forward rates, with columns for one, two, three, six and 12 months' forward. A premium is indicated when the left-hand figure is higher. For example, the dollar is quoted three months forward at a premium of 6/3 (0.06c-0.03c). A discount is indicated when the left-hand figure is lower.

10

Practical Guidelines for Forward Transactions

The guidelines in Chapter 5 for spot transactions are also appropriate for forward transactions. Additionally, for a large company or a bank with its own dealing room, there are other practical issues to consider when initiating a forward exchange transaction.

Preparing to Deal

The point was made in Chapter 5 that some simple preparation before starting to deal can help avoid costly mistakes. It is important to establish on which side of the spread transaction will be made, even more so than for spot transactions, since spreads widen in relation to the period to settlement. For example, if the spread for a dollar/sterling spot transaction is 10 points (one tenth of one cent) for a six-month forward transaction it might be, say, 15 points.

Selecting the Banks to Quote

Choosing which banks should be invited to quote requires more forethought for forward transaction (particularly long-dated) than for spot transactions. Although most banks are competitive for spot rate quotations, fewer are serious players in the forward market. This is primarily because of the amount of capital needed to run a forward book, but also because of the skills required. Most banks *will* quote a forward price but in many cases they will immediately "broke" the position on to a market-maker and retain a few basis points risk-free commission for themselves.

The dealer will get a better rate by going directly to the market-makers and eliminating intermediaries. For currencies such as the peseta, lira or French franc, the most obvious banks to use are the international banks of those countries, such as Banca Central Hispanoamericano or Banca Santander for Spain, Banco del Lavora or Credito Italiano for Italy, and Banque Nationale de Paris or Société Général for France. However, local banks might not always have the keenest prices and it may be better to include a few major market-makers such as Barclays, Citicorp or Deutsche Bank to ensure price competition.

Dealing

There are two components to a forward contract: the spot rate and the forward points. While the spot rate will continue to be volatile, with banks holding their quotes for a few seconds, the forward points are far less so, driven instead by more stable interest rate differentials.

A corporate dealer should seek the best prices by asking a number of banks to quote a premium or discount for a particular size and maturity of forward transaction. Banks will be willing to quote the forward points and hold their quotation for up to 15 minutes, giving the dealer time to assemble other quotes for price comparison. The dealer can then select the best forward points. The aggregate rate (of spot and discount or premium) is obtained by "agreeing" the spot with the bank. The spot rate element is transacted by asking the bank with the most competitive forward points to quote its spot rate and then comparing it to the reference rate shown on the screen. The dealer should tell the bank that the forward deal would only be transacted with that bank if its spot rate were acceptable.

Example

A dealer for a large multinational is looking for the best one-year forward rate for purchasing Swiss francs against sterling. He calls several banks in quick succession to request a quote of forward points. Each bank agrees to hold its quote for 15 minutes, giving him time to select the best offer. The quotes are as follows:

Bank X - 562 points, Bank Y - 565 points, Bank Z - 575 points.

Swiss interest rates are lower than in the UK, and so the forward points represent an additional cost and should be deducted from the sterling/ Swiss francs spot rate. The lowest quoted forward points give the most attractive quote, and the dealer should return to bank X and check the spot rate it is offering. If this is satisfactory, he will agree the quote and bring in the forward points (still on offer) to settle the forward rate for the transaction. For example, if Bank X quotes a spot rate of SFr2.20 =£1, the company will arrange a one-year forward contract at the spot rate minus the forward points, to obtain a forward rate of SFr2.1438= £1 (2.2000-0.0562).

Appendix: Currencies and their Liquidity

A list of some currencies and their Swift code identification, the core messaging system for processing financial services transactions worldwide, is given below. The legacy currencies of the EMU countries are being superseded by the euro. The Swift codes for these currencies are shown here.

Country	Currency	Swift Code
Algeria	dinar	DZD
Argentina	peso	ARP
Australia	Australian $	AUD
Austria (legacy currency*)	schilling	ATS
Belgium (legacy currency*)	Belgian franc	BEF
Bermuda	Bermuda $	BMD
Bolivia	Boliviano	BOP
Brazil	real	BRL
Bulgaria	lev	BGI
Burma	kyat	BUK
Canada	Canadian $	CAD
Cayman Is.	CI$	KYD
Cent. African Rep.	CFA franc	XAF
Chile	Chilean peso	CLP
Colombia	Colombian peso	COP
Congo (Dem Rep)	New zaire	ZRN

Country	Currency	Swift Code
Costa Rica	Colón	CRC
Cuba	Cuban peso	CUP
Cyprus	Cyprus £	CYP
Czech Republic	koruna	CSK
Denmark	Danish krone	DKK
Dominica	Dominican dollar	XCD
Dominican Rep.	peso	DOP
Ecuador	sucre	ECS
EMU	euro	EUR
Egypt	Egyptian £	EGP
Finland (legacy currency*)	markka	FIM
France (legacy currency*)	French franc	FRF
Germany (legacy currency*)	deutschemark	DEM
Great Britain	£ sterling	GBP
Greece	drachma	GRD
Haiti	gourde	HTG
Hong Kong	HK$	HKD
Hungary	forint	HUF
Iceland	Iceland krona	ISK
India	Indian rupee	INR
Indonesia	rupiah	IDR
Iran	rial	IRR
Irish Republic (legacy currency*)	Irish punt	IEP
Israel	new shekel	ILS
Italy (legacy currency*)	lira	ITL
Jamaica	Jamaican $	JMD
Japan	yen	JPY
Jordan	Jordan dinar	JOD

Country	Currency	Swift Code
Kenya	Kenya shilling	KES
Korea (South)	won	KRW
Kuwait	Kuwaiti dinar	KWD
Libya	Libyan dinar	LYD
Liechtenstein	Swiss franc	CHF
Luxembourg (legacy currency*)	Luxembourg franc	LUF
Malawi	kwacha	MWK
Malaysia	Ringgit/dollar	MYR
Malta	Maltese lira	MTP
Mexico	Mexican peso	MXN
Morocco	dirham	MAD
Netherlands (legacy currency*)	guilder	NLG
New Zealand	NZ$	NZD
Nigeria	naira	NGN
Norway	Norwegian krone	NOK
Pakistan	Pakistan rupee	PKR
Paraguay	guarani	PYG
Peru	new sol	PES
Philippines	Philippine peso	PHP
Poland	zloty	PLZ
Portugal (legacy currency*)	escudo	PTE
Romania	leu	ROL
Russia	rouble	SUR
Rwanda	Rwandan franc	RWF
Saudi Arabia	Saudi riyal	SAR
Singapore	Singaporean $	SGD
Slovakia	koruna	SKK
South Africa	rand	ZAR

Country	Currency	Swift Code
Spain (legacy currency*)	peseta	ESB
Sri Lanka	Sri Lanka rupee	LKR
Sweden	Swedish krona	SEK
Switzerland	Swiss franc	CHF
Syria	Syrian £	SYP
Taiwan	Taiwan $	TWD
Tanzania	Tanzanian shilling	TZS
Thailand	baht	THB
Trinidad/Tobago	Trin/Tob $	TTD
Tunisia	Tunisian dinar	TND
Turkey	Turkish lira	TRL
Uganda	shilling	UGX
United Kingdom	£ sterling	GBP
United States	US$	USD
Venezuela	bolivar	VEB
Vietnam	dong	VND
Zaire Rep	zaire	ZRN
Zambia	kwacha	ZMK
Zimbabwe	Zimbabwe $	ZWD

Liquidity in Currencies

A currency is said to be liquid if it is possible to buy or sell it easily in the FX markets, and at a reasonably priced rate.

The major traded currencies are liquid in all market centres, both spot and forward. The major currencies are currently (in order): the dollar, euro, yen and sterling. The most common trades are euro/dollar, dollar/yen, dollar/sterling, and dollar/Swiss franc. The dollar is one of the traded currencies in most FX transactions. Other liquid currencies are the euro, the Swiss franc, the British pound, the yen, the Australian dollar and the Canadian dollar. The volume of trading between particular currencies will vary from one market centre to another.

Some currencies are more liquid in some market centres than in others where demand and supply is much weaker. For example, prior to its replacement by the euro, the Italian lira was liquid during trading hours in Milan, London, Frankfurt and New York, but the market was generally thin in Asia. Similarly, the Spanish peseta was not very liquid outside Europe. Not surprisingly, currencies generally are traded most frequently in their own country. Only a few FX markets handle large volumes in a variety of currencies for banks and other customers around the world. The major centres are London, New York and Tokyo.

When a currency is liquid, the bid-offer spread will be narrower than if the currency were not liquid. This is evident in changes in bid-offer spreads during the course of a 24-hour day. The spot market for the Singaporean dollar, for example, is liquid during Singapore's trading hours, but outside these, the spread normally will widen. Similarly, the FX market for the Greek drachma is most liquid between 0730 and 1100 (GMT) each day.

A currency might have a liquid spot market, but a much less liquid forward market. Liquidity in the forward market varies according to the forward period of the contract. For example, a currency might be liquid forward up to six months, but not very liquid for longer periods. Even the forward market for sterling more than five years out is restricted to a small number of large banks, although forward contracts for sterling sometimes can be arranged up to 15 years. Banks will be more reluctant to deal forward in a weak or volatile currency because of the high risk of loss, unless they can square their position, that might not be easy in an illiquid market.

Liquidity in the forward market for a currency will vary between market centers. For example, the forward market for the Australian dollar is liquid out to five years in the Australian market, and forward contracts up to 10 years out are negotiable. Offshore, however, in London and Tokyo, most forward contracts in the Australian dollar are for three to six months, and the market is liquid out to only one year.

Currencies tend to be traded primarily with just a few other currencies. Most trades in the Canadian dollar, for example, are with the dollar. To find out how easy or difficult it is to arrange a spot or forward transaction in any particular currency, check a Reuters or Bloomberg screen where dealing banks will quote their prices, or ask your bank.

Liquidity in currencies continues to improve as international trade by those countries develops. To obtain the best price for a currency not heavily traded, it may be necessary to approach a few banks specialising in the currency. For example, Chase Manhattan specialises in the Indonesian rupiah, and only a few large banks deal forward more than five years out in the Italian lira. Domestic banks might be able to achieve 24-hour trading for their country's currency by opening offices in other markets around the world.

Glossary

Appreciation
Increase in the value of a currency against other currencies.

Bid Rate
The exchange rate at which a bank will sell a quoted or variable currency.
This is lower than the offer rate.

Broken Date
A settlement date for a forward contract that is not a standard number
of months – one, two, three, six or 12 – ahead. Also called an odd date.

Cable
Term for the sterling/dollar exchange rate.

Cash Market
Market for the purchase and sale of physical currencies, spot or forward.

Closeout
Cancellation of a forward contract involving a reverse FX transaction for
the same settlement date. For example, a company that has arranged a
forward contract to buy currency X from its bank can closeout the
contract at a later time by selling the same quantity of currency X for the
same value date to the bank.

Confirmation
Process of documenting an FX transaction to the other counterparty.

Convertible Currency
Currency that can be traded freely on the FX markets.

Cross Rate
Exchange rate between two currencies where neither is the dollar.

Dealing Date
The date on which a transaction is made.

Depreciation
Fall in the value of a currency against other currencies.

Discount
Amount by which a forward rate is cheaper than the spot rate. A forward rate is obtained by adding the discount to the spot rate.

Eurocurrency Rates
Interest rates for lending/depositing currency in the eurocurrency markets (short-term money markets).

Exposure
Being at risk of higher costs or lower income from a rise or fall in an exchange rate over a period of time that is referred to as the exposure period.

Extension
Rearrangement of a forward contract for settlement at a later date than originally agreed.

Forex
Abbreviation of foreign exchange.

Forward Contract
An FX transaction made now for the purchase or sale of a specified quantity of one currency in exchange for a second currency, at a

specified rate of exchange, for delivery and settlement at a date later than for spot transactions.

FX Swap

A buy-and-sell transaction involving a simultaneous agreement to buy or sell a quantity of currency on one date, or resell or repurchase the same quantity of currency at a different rate of exchange on another later date.

Hedge

An instrument or action for reducing risk.

Liquidity

The ease with which items can be bought or sold in the market. Liquidity in the spot and forward FX markets varies between currencies, countries and, sometimes the time of day. A liquid market means greater competition among banks for business and consequently keener prices and smaller spreads.

Long Position

Dealing position in which a dealer, e.g. a bank, has bought more of an item, e.g. currency, than has been sold for a given value date.

Odd Date

See Broken Date

Offer Rate

The exchange rate at which a bank will offer to buy a quoted or variable currency. This is higher than the bid rate.

Overnight

A short-dated buy-and-sell transaction involving the sale or purchase of currency for value today and the repurchase or resale of the currency for value tomorrow.

Points

Smallest unit of measurement for exchange rates. For the dollar/sterling rate, for example, a point is $0.0001, 0.01 cents.

Premium

Amount by which a forward rate is more expensive than the spot rate. A forward rate is obtained by deducting the premium from the spot rate.

Settlement Date

See Value Date

Short Position

Dealing position in which a dealer has sold more of an item than has been bought for a given value date.

Spot-Next

A buy-and-sell transaction made today involving the sale or purchase of currency for value in two days' time and the repurchase or resale of the currency for value on the day following.

Spot Rate (Interbank Spot Rate)

The exchange rate for a large FX transaction between two banks for settlement in two working days. Very large companies also might obtain interbank spot rates. Rates for smaller spot transactions will be based on interbank spot rates, but bid rates will be lower and offer rates higher.

Spot Transaction

An FX transaction made now for the immediate purchase or sale of a specified quantity of one currency in exchange for a second currency. The actual exchange of currencies takes place two working days later, on spot value date.

Spread

Difference between bid and offer rates.

Square Position
Dealing position in which a dealer, e.g. a bank, has bought and sold equal amounts of an item, e.g. a currency, for a given value date.

Swift Code
An international code for identifying currencies.

Tom-next
A short-dated buy-and-sell transaction made today involving the sale or purchase of currency for value tomorrow and the repurchase or resale of the currency for value on the day following.

Value Date
The settlement date on which the exchange of currencies takes place, and the buyer receives the value for the currency position.

Value Date Option Contract
Forward contract in which the customer has some choice of value date between an earliest and latest specified date, i.e., some choice in deciding when to buy or sell the currency.

Index